MESSIAH - A New Look at the Composer, the Music and the Message

MESSIAH! ✡

A NEW LOOK AT THE COMPOSER, THE MUSIC AND THE MESSAGE!

By

N. A. Woychuk, M.A., Th.D.

Author, You Need to Memorize Scripture,
forty-three memory books for all age levels,
numerous other books and Bible games.

Foreword by

Dr. Alfred B. Smith

Indexes by

Gladys Teague

Sc: _____ wship

P.O. _____ 63141

Messiah - A New Look at the Composer,
the Music and the Message

© 1995 by N. A. Woychuk

ISBN 1-880960-26-5

Library of Congress Catalog Card
Number 95-68353

Cover by Glenn Myers © 1995

Printed in the United States of America

Photo Illustrations

Contents of Biography

Contents of Commentary and Music

George Frideric Handel after a portrait by Thomas Hudson, 1747.

Foreword

In the early nineteenth century, Beethoven (1770-1827) called Handel "the greatest and most able composer that ever lived."

Almost eighty-five years later, in 1894, editor Frederick Crowest wrote, "Handel's masterpiece has probably done more to convince mankind that there is a God above us than all of the theological works ever written."

How is it that even today this text and musical composition written some two hundred fifty years ago still continues to attract an ever-increasing number of enthusiastic performers and appreciative listeners?

To help find the answer to this challenging question and to shed some invaluable light on this God-honored "masterpiece" is the main objective of my friend, N. A. Woychuk in writing this timely book.

You will be both thrilled and spiritually challenged as he retraces the life of Handel from his youthful and formative days in Germany and eventually to the times of acclaim and adulation in England as one of the world's great and most famous composers. A life that you will discover had its valleys as well as its peaks, its disappointments as well as its joys.

I'm happy that my friend included this revealing biography, for in it I discern the providential hand of the "Master Potter" as He molds and shapes a vessel for His special use.

More excitement is also in store as we are introduced to Charles Jennens and the important part he played in this whole drama of redemption. Someone has said that, "had there not been a Charles Jennens who did the groundwork and presented Handel with the folder containing the seventy-nine Scripture verses, there never would have been the great *Messiah*." And neither would there have been this factual and enjoyable treatise you are about to read, if it had not been for the years of diligent "groundwork" done by its author, Dr. N. A. Woychuk.

Dr. Woychuk's life and work has been saturated with the Bible. His involvement has not only been in preaching and teaching the WORD, but he has authored numerous books which encourage and instruct, particularly families, on how to memorize and understand the Bible.

In the early part of his ministry, he was led to found an organization which gave form and purpose to his heart's desire that "all should hide God's Word in their hearts."

He is still very actively engaged as its director. Only eternity will reveal the untold thousands who have been fortified for this life and for eternity by Scripture Memory Fellowship.

From this background, I am sure you can see why I have the confidence in his writing ability that I do.

It was Handel himself who said that he had succeeded in writing what he did because the words were God's words and "they seemed to sing by themselves." Enough books have been written about the music of the *Messiah* to fill a library, but much of the interpretation of God's Word has been rather inaccurate and in many cases ignored. Dr. Woychuk has done much to shed light on these inaccuracies and omissions; for this he is to be highly commended.

I could go on, but time forbids because I would not want to deprive you of the extra moments of spiritual blessing and enjoyment that is awaiting you as you begin this "Adventure In Inspiration."

God bless you . . .

"Sing"cerely,

Alfred B. Smith

For I know that my Redeemer liveth, and that He shall stand at the latter day upon the earth:

And though after my skin worms destroy this body, yet in my flesh shall I see God. (Job 19:25)

Preface

Two hundred fifty-four years ago, timeless words were suitably united with matchless music; in the hands of George Frideric Handel, this felicitous union became the enduring creation called *Messiah*.

In 1958, I spent the month of November in London and Glasgow on a mission of securing good Christian books for rewards in the ministry of Bible memorizing. All of my spare hours were spent in used book stores. On the third story of one, I came across some twenty large volumes of a Christian magazine bound annually in hardback covers, dating back almost one hundred years.

On the return trip on the S.S. United States, I spent many profitable hours during those five wonderful days over the Atlantic in a cursory examination of those volumes. In the 1894 edition, I read the article on Handel and *Messiah*. On arriving home, it was filed in an appropriate folder for future consideration.

It appears on page one in introducing this biography.

As the tri-centennial anniversary of Handel's birth was approaching some ten years ago, I spent a few days at the Library of Congress in Washington D.C. and then wrote a short biography of George Frideric Handel, the composer of the oratorio *Messiah*.

Almost two years ago, the matter of Handel and *Messiah* was undertaken in deep earnest and with the clear conviction that it was of the Lord.

The task is now complete, including a thirteen chapter biography of Handel from the viewpoint of a believer, a fifteen chapter commentary on the Scriptures of the oratorio and helpful comments on the music itself. In retrospect, the hand of the Lord is seen in unusual and numerous ways over a period of decades which to relate in full would call for another book.

The amazing story of Handel and *Messiah* has now been finalized, and the only deduction is the fact that many of His servants prayed in earnest, and the prayer-answering God enabled the unique endeavor to be achieved at this time. There is high expectation that the book will have a fruitful ministry in various directions as it travels along with Handel's *Messiah*.

It seems incredible that an effort such as this was not undertaken a century or two earlier. Over one hundred books have been published on Handel and *Messiah* during the twentieth century, but none, so far as is known, from the Christian point of view.

The hidden purpose of this undertaking is that it should become a warm invitation and an inescapable challenge to memorize all the Scriptures in this immortal oratorio. This will lead to inestimable blessing in the life of each one who does it. For those who will pursue this, a handy booklet with just the seventy-nine Bible verses is available.

What more can be said except to encourage all who read it to engage in heartful praise to God. And in praying for the ministry of the book, one would desire first of all that "it shall be to the Lord for a name" (Isa. 55:13), for a lasting memorial to our wonderful, living Messiah!

There is a deep sense of appreciation to God for the many who have helpfully participated in this effort in numerous and sundry ways. Reading the manuscript at the beginning included Bob and Gladys Teague, Steve and Sandra Walker, Paul and Marcia Daniels and Sharon Woychuk Goodman. Dr. Ruth M. Kantzer studied the subject and then followed it up with numerous choice suggestions. Gladys Teague prepared the three indexes which involved many days in pursuing diligently the labor of love. Further reading of the manuscript included Diane King Susek.

Dr. Alfred B. Smith, an eminent musician and a personal friend, not only wrote the foreword, but also shared in vital decisions relating to the printing of the book.

Dorothy Grant and Debbie Wagner, SMF staff members, did splendid work in setting the type and the endless proofreading. The greatest measure of appreciation must go to my son Jim who, from the beginning, was the chief helper, counselor and encourager. The list fails to include all those who prayed, all those who sent words of encouragement and those faithful friends who graciously sent of their substance for the printing of the book. Deep gratitude is expressed to everyone who, in any way, has shared in this endeavor.

"This is the Lord's doing; it is marvelous in our eyes!" (Ps. 118:23).

March 1, 1995   N. A. Woychuk
                                 St. Louis, Missouri

Seating in the great Crystal Palace at the performance of *Messiah*

Chapter 1

Messiah's
Enduring Greatness

In 1894—one hundred fifty-three years after *Messiah* was composed—a festival in honor of Handel and his immortal *Messiah* was celebrated at the Crystal Palace[1] in London.

The full chorus of *Messiah* consisted of 2,997 voices picked from various cathedrals and other choirs from all over the country.

In its July issue of that year, the *Christian Treasury*, a magazine in London, carried this report:

> The vast crowd is hushed. Silent, breathless—every note writes its expression on every face. The genius of the composer levels all distinctions of rank and class, of culture and intellect. The listeners are all absorbed. There is no affectation or pretence about it. What do the great majority in the crowd care about canons of musical culture? What do they

---

[1]The Crystal Palace—a place of wonder for an amazing event. All iron girders, the all glass conservatory covered twenty acres of London's Hyde Park. It was taken down two years later and rebuilt in southeast London. Handel festivals were held in the Crystal Palace until 1936, when it was consumed in a spectacular fire.

know whether it is the right sort of thing, or the wrong sort of thing to be delighted by the music of Handel? They only know that they feel it; that they cannot help feeling it; that they are drawn unto the heaven of heavens by it.

Handel's music speaks to us of things that in all our lives we have not known, and in life can never know. It lifts us out of the sordid world of petty strivings and foolish rivalries, and carries us into the purer and higher air where the yearnings are at least for the moment satisfied to the most exquisite fulness . . .

Such an exalted experience is hard to describe or to grasp. Speaking more pragmatically of the "spiritual power which *Messiah* has exercised over thousands upon thousands in all civilized lands," Frederick J. Crowest asserted in that same year—1894—that Handel's masterpiece "is the most powerful of all civilizing agencies," since its music "has probably done more to convince thousands of mankind that there is a God about us than all the theological works ever written."

Though the sweeping conclusion of Mr. Crowest is subject to challenge, we must readily confess that for those whose hearts are tuned to the Redeemer's praise, this musical rendition of some fifty portions of Scripture affords one of the noblest gratifications of which we are capable in the present life.

The *Messiah* of Handel consists of three parts. The first contains the remarkable prophecies of His coming, and the blessed consequences, together with the angel's message to the shepherds, informing them of His birth, as related by Luke.

The second part carries the major aspect of our Lord's mission. It takes in His indescribable sufferings, His vicarious death and His glorious resurrection, and

His triumph over sin and death. The thunderous outburst of the Hallelujah Chorus sweeps us heavenward.

The third part fittingly begins with the sweet, satisfying words of Job, who amidst all his suffering and
confusion assures us that "Redeemer liveth." In this
section we are told the results of Messiah's undertaking, and the transformation of all believers into immortality and incorruption at the sound of the trumpet
and the coming of the Lord. It closes with the hallelujahs, the new song of the redeemed and the unending
Amen.

Messiah, the major theme of the oratorio, is the
leading principal subject of all the Scriptures. All the
aspects of His mediatorial work as Savior are covered
in the seventy-nine Bible verses that make up the
composition. Complete salvation becomes available
to all mankind as a direct result of our Lord's victory
over all the strongholds of sin and death. This epic
could almost be as appropriately called *Redemption*
though it is better that it bears the name of the wonderful Redeemer through whom redemption has been
made available for all.

H. A. Streatfeild describes *Messiah* in his biography
of Handel as "not only a very great work of art, but . . .
actually the first instance in the history of music of an
attempt to view the mighty drama of redemption from
an artistic standpoint."

It is interesting, though sad, that so many of the
biographers of Handel fail to comprehend the meaning and scope of the Scriptures in the oratorio and the
unique development of redemption that they convey.

Paul Henry Lang, author of numerous fine musical
studies, wrote one of the most complete and salutary
biographies of Handel. But he is certainly wide of the
mark when he states that "The Deity that finally
emerges from this great work is the triumphant God

of the Old Testament whom Handel so often praised in his oratorios, not Christ the redeemer, whom he so magnificently evokes in one of his arias—and this in spite of the fact that *Messiah* is essentially a paean of Redemption."

Lang somehow fails to see the Redeemer in almost every one of the Old Testament Scriptures. They are the inspired, prophetic and direct revelations of Christ and His sufferings. The historical Christ of the New Testament is but the fulfillment of the Old Testament predictions concerning Him.

In a similar vein, another biographer, the distinguished Cambridge scholar, Richard Luckett, complains that the Scripture texts in *Messiah* are "wrenched from their context," and that Jennens, the man who compiled the Scriptures, "implied applications that were not justified."

Mr. Luckett's observations are incorrect. John Newton (1725-1807), the highly esteemed hymn writer and pastor of the Church of England Parish Church of St. Mary Woolnoth, preached fifty discourses in 1784 and 1785, covering all the Scripture passages which form the subject of the oratorio. Mr. Newton accepted the Messianic application of the Old Testament passages. He objected to the character of the performers and to the kind of people who generally flocked to hear the performance.

If anything was not entirely correct with the choice of the Scriptures or with their sequence in the compilation, Mr. Newton was fully qualified to notice it, and he would have been the first one to proclaim it. On the contrary, he praised the selection and the sequence of those Scriptures. Hear his remarks in his first discourse: "The arrangement or series of these passages is so judiciously disposed, so well connected and so fully comprehends all the principal truths of the gospel, that I shall not attempt to alter or to enlarge it."

Handel, who knew the Scriptures well, found no problem with the Jennens compilation. Scholars in every generation who believe implicitly that the Bible in its entirety is the inspired, unerring Word of God, find no difficulty with the coherence of the Scriptures in this composition. Indeed, it is the wise selection and arrangement of those Scriptures that in no small measure accounts for the greatness of the *Messiah*.

Handel composed fifty operas, twenty-three oratorios and many other outstanding compositions, but the one that has held the attention of the world for more than two and a half centuries is the sacred oratorio *Messiah*. It has become a universal favorite, a household familiarity.

Scores of good biographies of Handel have been written. Numerous worthy studies and analyses have been made of his magnificent compositions. Handel's use of musical figures that have a pictorial quality to express graphic images is suggested. He wrote singable music for particular voices. He composed instrumental arrangements that were playable. He made the best use of melody, harmony, volume and rhythm. Yes, but what else is it that makes *Messiah* live on? One scholar advances the idea that the secret of Handel's genius may be the "unique blend of the fulness and majesty of the *German* music, the delicacy and elegance of the *Italian* and the solidity of the *English*." Another adds to that blend "the grace of the *French* music."

All these are noteworthy, but we are still left wondering what it is in this composition that lifts us into such inner satisfaction. What is it that so strangely captivates our full attention and edifies our hearts? There is no dramatic action, no plot, no narrative. Even the recitatives and arias are undramatic. Where-

6

in, therefore, lies its enduring power? What is the secret of *Messiah's* immortality?

The answer to those questions is the object of this effort.

Peter Jacobi ponders its powerful effect: " 'Handel deals with ideas,' as Streatfeild says, and perhaps that is the reason for our loving acceptance of *Messiah*. In the work, through it, by it, we are transported out of our care-ridden existences. We can close our eyes, and as our ears take in those beautiful melodies, we can receive very personal visions of something better, something more important than what surrounds and concerns us."

Chapter 2

Impressive
Musical Beginnings

Georg Friedrich Handel was born February 23, 1685 in Halle, Saxony, in eastern Germany, the second child of his father's second marriage to a pastor's daughter thirty years younger. His father George was a barber-surgeon by profession. This odd double profession was somewhat common at the time. To indulge a pun—perhaps the razor could be readily turned in the performance of either profession. However, the knife was not as commonly used by surgeons as it is now.

We have an interesting record of the doctor's operation on Andreas Rudeluff, a sixteen-year-old peasant boy, who in the course of playing with his friends, swallowed a knife with a staghorn handle. The long operation was slow and painful. First magnetic plasters were used. On June 18, 1692, the doctor managed to fasten a silk thread to the knife. Slowly, step by perilous and painful step, he pulled the knife out of Andreas' stomach. It had been there for five hundred and thirty days. Andreas, we are told, rejoiced and praised the Lord.

The odd "operation" notwithstanding, George

Handel was one of the most renowned doctors in Germany and always a welcome guest at the princely courts surrounding Halle. He was a man of strength, self-discipline and courage.

Georg Friedrich's mother, Dorothea, came from a long line of Lutheran pastors. She was a good and godly woman whom Handel remembered with warm affection.

Handel showed a remarkable love for music from his earliest years. He took part in the singing at the grammar school, and heard the music in Our Lady's Lutheran Church, where the family worshipped regularly. His father, though not disliking music, was eager for his son to become a lawyer. The boy's musical inclinations were not particularly encouraged until his Aunt Anna came to live with them.

One day upon arrival from school he found a clavichord (an early stringed keyboard instrument similar to the spinet) in his room. No one admitted procuring it, but Friedrich knew that it was the thoughtful aunt. The father was outraged and asked that the instrument be removed at once, but was entreated otherwise when the boy pleaded with him and stated that he had to practice music for school.

The Strong Influence of Pietism

The Lutheran Church in the early seventeenth century remained orthodox, but the spiritual element was weak. The emphasis was "upon pure doctrine and the Sacraments as the constituent elements of the Christian life. The layman's role was the entirely passive one of accepting the dogmas and remaining loyal to the church" (John Weinlick). The Catholic leadership was anemic, well characterized by H. G. Wells as "weak popes, declining monasteries and lazy bishops." Furthermore, the rationalism of the philosophers in the "Age of Reason" created a further deadening effect upon the churches.

The Thirty Years' War (1618-48) created, among other negative factors, a serious moral and spiritual deterioration, and this awakened widespread interest in the earlier devotional literature which the pietists were promoting. The writings of Johannes Tauler (1300-61) and other German, Dutch and even Spanish authors were again in demand. Influences from revived English puritanism were reaching the Continent in such writings as Richard Baxter's (1615-91) *A Call to the Unconverted,* Lewis Bayly's (1565-1631) *The Practice of Piety* and John Bunyan's (1628-88) *Pilgrim's Progress.*

It was at this juncture when pietism became a strong factor in Christendom. This movement gave renewed attention to the role of the Scriptures in Christianity. They regarded the Bible as not only the source of Christian doctrine, but it was the source of the spiritual life as well. Pietism was inherently a "protest" movement in its opposition to the weakening protestant "establishment." Tracing out the progress of this movement is vital in learning how much influence it had on the aspiring young musician.

The various streams of concern for renewal converged in the life and work of Philipp J. Spener (1635-1705) in different parts of Germany. His messages urged repentance and renewal. Spiritual life classes for children and adults were held on each Sunday afternoon. Meetings were held each Sunday and Wednesday at Spener's home. This practice flourished and spread, and those who attended such "conventicles" began to be called Pietists.

August Hermann Francke (1663-1727), whom Spener met at the Saxon University in Leipzig, became in a sense Spener's successor in the pietist movement. With the aid of King Frederick I of Prussia, a new university was founded at Halle in 1694 and Francke became professor of oriental languages and theology. In addition, Francke organized numerous institutions and business enterprises, including an orphanage and a Paedagogium.

It is interesting to learn that Count Nicholaus Von Zinzendorf, the devout Moravian leader, attended Francke's Academy for several years, beginning in 1710. It was Zinzendorf who formulated the slogan which played such a great role in the history of revivals: "Come as you are. It is only necessary to believe in the atonement of Christ."

Spiritual revival swept across Saxony, and Halle became the center of piety and missionary enthusiasm. It is for this reason, perhaps, that the Handels and the Tausts (Mrs. Handel's family) moved there "for the love of pure evangelical truth." This appears in biographies, but no source for it can be established.

The Visit to Weissenfels

Friedrich seldom ventured out into the streets of Halle with other boys. He spent most of his spare time with his music and his dreams. He was really excited when his father somewhat reluctantly took him to Weissenfels, some twenty miles from Halle. There, his Uncle Christian took him to church on Sundays. The organist noticed the lad's keen interest in organ music. During rehearsal time one day, Friedrich asked hesitatingly, "May I try to play it?"

The organist was amazed at how the nine-year-old boy improvised a melody on the large organ. "The Duke must hear this," he said. Next Sunday, His Grace the Duke of Saxe-Weissenfels listened attentively as the chords rang out from the small hands of the boy. "Your son is abnormally gifted," the Duke told his father. "We have never heard a child play in such a remarkable manner. He must be trained." Friedrich's heart leaped with joy, but the father countered firmly, "I want my boy to study law, and not be distracted from his destiny by music."

The Duke persisted, however, "God gave him this talent; it is not for you to ignore it. Your son must be taught music." While the subdued father stood speechless, the gracious Duke took a handful of coins from his pocket, gave them to Friedrich and said, "Remember, you earned the first money with music, my boy."

Both the boy and the father must have long remembered the words, "God gave him this talent."

His father could not forget the Duke's strong words. After considerable delay, he finally arranged music lessons for Friedrich "so long as it did not conflict with his school work." The music instructor was Friedrick Wilhelm Zachow (also spelled Zachau), an able composer-organist of the Liebfrauenkirche and director of the town choir. Zachow was a distinguished musician and a gracious teacher of both composition and performance.

Handel received from his imaginative teacher a "solid grounding in harmony, counterpoint, and choral writing, as well as in imaginative orchestration." Zachow also instilled in his student an intellectual curiosity regarding the various styles of music from those whom he considered to be among the greatest Italian and German composers without directing his attention particularly to any one of them. He wisely left Handel to form a style of his own.

The solid training Handel received from Zachow formed his musical aspirations for life. Handel's appreciation for his teacher was enormous. After Zachow's death in 1712, Handel, by then the famous London composer, "sent frequent remittances to his widow."

Zachow had an unusually fine library of music. Handel perused many volumes, and in those impressionable years, he absorbed a comprehensive knowledge of the styles and techniques of great musicians. By the time Handel was eleven, he could play the organ, the piano, the violin and the oboe.

A Trip to Berlin

Information on dates and travels during these years is somewhat inconclusive, but it appears that in 1696, Handel made a trip to Berlin. Zachow encouraged it and offered to go there with him. After weeks of persuasion, the father gave permission, but in doing so he said, "Give me your word, son, that sooner or later you will study at the University here in Halle, no matter what happens."

After the ten-day trip, Friedrich and Zachow reached Berlin. Zachow learned that none other than the Electress Sophia Charlotte, who had heard of the child prodigy, had invited him to play at the court. The concert was advertised all over the city. Though Handel was frightened, he sat at the organ and performed amazingly well before the elegant audience. It all seemed like a dream.

Like the Duke of Weissenfels, the Elector Frederick III (later King Frederick I of Prussia) was deeply impressed, and at once offered to provide for the boy's musical education, including studies in Italy, the music capital of the world at the time. Friedrich was delighted and could hardly believe it. His joy was cut short when his father expressed his negative attitude and asked that the boy should return home at once. With his shattered dreams behind him, Friedrich went back to school in obedience to his father who admonished him, "Put not your trust in princes!"

His Father's Death

Friedrich's father became very ill and died on February 11, 1697 when the boy was scarcely twelve years old. He stood silently by his father's coffin and determined to keep the pledge he had made to enter law school. He wrote a poem in memory of his father, whom he highly respected despite their differences. The concluding lines of the poem reveal a little of the boy's spiritual progress:

God, who relieves me of a father's care
By that dear father's death, yet liveth still;
And henceforth in my anguish and despair,
I find my help and guidance in His will.

For the next few years, the records are not clear as to what Handel was doing. We know that he continued his studies in music, likely on his own. He may have made another trip to Berlin.

The University Contacts

Desiring to fulfill his father's wishes, Handel matriculated at Halle University on February 10, 1702, but the boisterous life style at the University did not appeal to his sensitive nature. He enjoyed meeting some outstanding musicians, including composer Philip Telemann and Barthold Brockes.

It is probable that Handel may have had some contact with Professor Francke, leader of the pietist movement, though no record of any such association seems to exist. However, the pietist influence is seen in a number of Handel's works, "coloring the mood of the late oratorios such as *Susanna* and *Theodora* and traceable even in *Messiah*."[1]

We know that Handel's mother, Dorothea, exemplified an earnest piety and an intimate acquaintance with the text and teaching of the Holy Scriptures, qualities which she sought faithfully to inculcate into the

---

[1] Jonathan Keates in his recent Handel biography.

character of her children. Handel's understanding and love of the Scriptures came from the teaching of his mother and the pietist influences at the university. In surveying the life of Handel, there seems to be no other place or time in his life where such influences existed.

In addition to his post at the University, Professor Francke operated a Bible Academy, and was also particularly devoted to the care of deserted children and orphans. His Foundling Hospital (a home for deserted children) was used as a model in many countries. Young Handel was deeply impressed by this effort and this likely influenced his keen interest in the Foundling Hospital in London many years later.

Conditions at the University progressively deteriorated. The serious riots and other problems caused King Frederick I to drop Halle from the list of universities which he supported. This action brought about the school's rapid decline. It became obvious that it was no longer the place for young Handel.

When he was at a loss to know what to do, an opportunity was offered him to serve as organist of the Reformed Calvinistic Cathedral. He was then seventeen years of age. The salary was small but the experience of playing and maintaining the organ was invaluable. The contract was for one year.

The Hamburg Adventure

By this time Handel began to feel sure of himself and conscious of his musical abilities. When his contract as organist expired, Handel packed his few belongings, bade farewell to his mother and family, and at the age of eighteen he headed for Hamburg, which at that time was the operatic center of Germany. Opera was beginning to call Handel in an evermore insistent voice.

Almost upon arrival there, he met Johann Mattheson, who, though only four years older, was proficient in music and was already singing in the opera. They exchanged lessons; Handel taught Mattheson counterpoint, Mattheson taught Handel the dramatic style. They went together to Lubeck to compete for the post of organist there in succession to the famous Buxtehude, but one of the conditions for securing the job was marriage to Buxtehude's unattractive daughter. They both declined the offer as did J. S. Bach sometime later.

Handel evidently had a dry sense of humor and "behaved as though he didn't know how many beans made a dozen" wrote Mattheson some years later. The two men had a quarrel which might have brought serious consequences, but they settled the matter and remained friends for the rest of their lives.

Rich in musical talent and constrained by good intentions, Handel was soon given a post as second violin at the Hamburg Opera House.

A certain poet named Feustking, who wrote librettos for the Hamburg Opera, gave Handel a strange libretto to set to music, entitled *Almira*. Little more than a week later, it was performed, with Mattheson as the principal tenor. Handel felt overwhelmed with success. His first opera, *Almira*, was a remarkable achievement, and Handel, though still inexperienced, already had developed an "aural imagination" whereby the music sounds well because it is deliberately planned to match the sound values of the words. This was something that Mattheson had noticed and admired, and often imitated in his own compositions.

Almira ran continually for some twenty nights, and Handel was suddenly recognized as a famous composer. He pursued his work zealously, although he did take time to teach harpsichord to the son of the

British consul in Hamburg, Sir John Wich. The consul was highly pleased with the young musician and said, "Some day you must come to London."

Following that, Handel said, "My inclination was always to go to England."

Chapter 3

Italy's Musical Influence

Italy, in Handel's time, was the cradle of opera, oratorio and concerto. To musicians, artists and poets, Italy was the radiant center of the world.

Prince Ferdinand de' Medici of Florence urged Handel to travel and study in Italy. He went so far as to offer to take care of expenses incurred in such travel. The Prince was very much of the same persuasion as Dr. Samuel Johnson who said, "that a man who has not been to Italy is always conscious of an inferiority, from his not having seen what it is expected a man should see. The grand object of travelling is to see the shores of the Mediterranean" (quoted by Christopher Hogwood).

Handel seriously considered studying music in Italy, but being of an independent mind and not wishing to impose on another person, he would not accept the offer of the kindhearted Prince. He planned to go to Italy as soon as he could save enough money.

It was his intention to visit every place in Italy which was known for its musical performances.

17

His first stop was the soul-inspiring Florence, which in the simple grandeur of its Tuscan architecture, was the most beautiful of cities. Lorenzo de Medici (1449-92), an astute politician, poet and scholar, was the leading figure in the Italian Renaissance, and made Florence one of the richest and most powerful city-states in Europe. It possessed the choicest treasures of statuary and painting by the greatest masters the world had ever seen. It was the birthplace of Dante (1265-1321), of Michelangelo (1475-1564) and was the scene of the most dramatic adventures in the Italian story. What person such as Handel could breathe the very air of Florence and not feel the exhilaration of the sights!

We do not know how long Handel stayed in Florence on his first visit there. We know that he arrived in Rome in January of 1707. This is recorded in "Diario do Roma" by Francesco Valesio. In his entry for January 14, 1707 we find unmistakable evidence: "There has arrived in this city a Saxon who is an excellent harpsichord player and composer of music who today exhibited his prowess by playing the organ at St. John Lateran to the astonishment of everybody."

At that time, Rome had about 150,000 inhabitants, a labyrinth of narrow streets, houses of extreme antiquity, monasteries, nunneries, and a series of great churches—with St. Peter's as the foremost one.

Handel acquired at once the enthusiastic interest of three Roman Catholic cardinals—Pietro Ottoboni, Carlo Colonna and Benedetto Panfili. In his association with Cardinal Ottoboni and his music group, Handel made a significant contact with the orchestra leader, Arcangelo Corelli. He learned from him the technique of controlling an orchestra so as to produce a clean sound. Corelli's precision and insistence on the highest professional standards deeply impressed Handel.

Handel's first protector in Rome was Cardinal Colonna, and Ruspoli was his chief Roman patron. He was expected to provide music, especially Italian cantatas, for the Sunday morning concerts not only in Rome but elsewhere as well.

When Handel first came to Italy, the masters of music in greatest esteem were Alessandro Scarlatti, Gasparini and Lotti. Scarlatti's son, Dominico, was so struck with Handel's unusual method of playing the harpsichord and organ, that he followed him all over Italy.

Back in Florence, Handel composed *Rodrigo*, his first Italian opera, and it was performed there in the early autumn of 1707. He spent two winters in Venice where his new opera *Agrippina* was composed and performed for twenty-seven successive nights to enthusiastic audiences.

Upon returning to Rome and the Ruspoli court, he composed the oratorio *La Resurrezione*. It was a great success and received much commendation from the musical elite. Handel's ability to project his music effectively into the female roles was demonstrated in this composition. The leading part in this oratorio is the figure of Mary Magdalene, and Handel composed a strikingly beautiful melody for Signora Durastanto who carried that part.

During his sojourn in Italy, influence was tactfully exerted to turn the young musician to Roman Catholicism, but he was resolute in remaining a Lutheran.

Wherever Handel's operas and oratorios were performed, the listeners were thunderstruck "with the grandeur and sublimity of his style." Till then, they had never known the powers of harmony and modulation so closely arrayed, and so forcibly combined. His performances were usually greeted with cries of "Viva il caro Sassone" ("Long live the beloved Saxon").

God forms the diamond but man must work upon it 'ere it can give forth its full lustre. Handel accepted this premise and gave much of his time to diligent work and practice. He acquired a sure mastery of the Italian opera and the graceful, flowing melodic style of the Italian music. His social education was also greatly enhanced. He discovered how people at court lived, ate and drank and made conversation. In short, "he arrived in Italy a gifted but crude composer with an uncertain command of form," writes Winton Dean, "and left it a polished and fully equipped artist."

The music at this time was generally "the new style of the Baroque, with an emphasis on the solo voice, clarity of text, polarity between the melody and bass line, and an interest in expressive harmony." Handel went to Italy in quest of modern music at its best, and although he learned a great deal from his years there, he became frustrated by certain aspects of Italy's musical dominance.

He composed over one hundred Italian cantatas, some of vast length, chamber music duets and trios, two oratorios, and two operas.

He scrutinized carefully the reigning musical tendencies as well as the cultural and social graces in the highest stratum of Italian society, but he sensed, as a whole, a tendency contrary to his ideals and emotional depths. Having observed the range of Italian music and having acquired a greater confidence in his own powers to create a music world of his own, he would now seek to determine the country where he could effectively build such a domain.

Chapter 4

"I Must Go to England"

Early in 1710, when Handel was conducting his opera in Venice, Ernest Augustus, the Prince of Hanover, Germany, seated near the stage, was delighted with the young musician and said to him, "Your conducting has pleased me very much Herr Handel; I would be glad if you would return with me to Hanover to take charge of music at my court." Handel gladly accepted the offer. He remained director of music at Hanover until 1716, though most of the time it was *in absentia*.

A few months thereafter he felt compelled to leave. He spoke with the Prince, "Your Highness, I beg permission to leave the court for a little time, for I must go to England." The Prince, who later became England's King George I encouraged such a visit, though it was with the understanding that Handel would officially remain the director of music at Hanover.

Quick Visit Home

On his way to England, Handel stopped over at Halle to visit his family. It was a warm and loving

21

Portrait of Handel,
after painting by
Bartholomew
Dandridge, probably
about the time
Handel settled
in London

Charles Jennens,
librettist, compiled
the libretto (text) for
the *Messiah*

reunion with the son, no longer the stripling who set out for Hamburg, but a distinguished looking young man. Filial devotion was one of the most prominent traits in Handel's character.

Much had happened at the old home place. His youngest sister, Johanna Christiana, had died and his elder sister, Dorothea Sophia, had married a prominent member of the Prussian Imperial Service. His mother and his Aunt Anna lived alone and the house looked more empty and more gloomy than ever. Their lives were those of simple piety, and although they could not fully grasp the magnitude of the son's world of music, they must have felt amply rewarded for the encouragement they gave him in his early years.

Georg Friedrich Handel arrived in London sometime late in 1710. At this time in London, the rich were enormously rich and powerful, the poor "terribly degraded, the middle class small and unstable. Nonconformists and Catholics lived under intermittently crippling restrictions" (H. C. Robbins Landon).

Handel could hardly speak a word of English, but he plunged at once into the pursuit of composing music for the London audiences. The English loved music, but a curious state of confusion existed. Crime was prevalent and people were reluctant to venture out at night. Operas failed one after another. Critics raged—especially against the Italian operas.

"Music Just Poured Out of Me"

Handel established contact with Aaron Hill, who was operating the Queen's Theatre in the Haymarket. Hill knew that there was something wrong with the music that was being offered. He summoned Handel to the theatre, gave him a copy of a play by a wandering Italian named Giacomo Rossi, and asked to see what he could do with it. Handel accepted the challenge and put his whole heart into it.

He said later, "The music just poured out of me." Soon his sparkling opera, *Rinaldo*, was born, and aroused considerable enthusiasm among the English when performed in early 1711. Some called *Rinaldo* a "masterpiece." The crowds kept coming and *Rinaldo* was played fifteen times between February and June. His rich melodies and his stirring harmonies were the talk of the town and he was suddenly the most famous composer in London.

New Citizenship—New Responsibility

Recognizing his responsibility to the Prince of Hanover, Handel returned there a number of times. In 1714, upon the death of British Queen Anne, Ernest Augustus, the Prince of Hanover, became King George I of England. For a while he seemed to keep Handel at a distance, much to the dismay of the young musician whom the Elector had formerly befriended. But Handel may have simply imagined this because the King happily listened to music by Handel in his chapel a few days after his arrival in London. Soon thereafter he heard *Rinaldo* at the opera house. Furthermore, he increased the general annual payment to Handel which Queen Anne had made; it was increased again a few years later when Handel became harpsichord teacher to the royal princesses.

In 1717, a concert was being planned and Handel was called upon to arrange the entire festivity. Handel's composition was performed by a fifty-piece orchestra at an entertainment place by the river Thames, hence its name— *Water Music*. The King was so pleased with it that he requested that the concert be repeated after supper.

Though still not generally accepted by the English, Handel did feel more secure, and, therefore, purchased a house at 57 Lower Brook Street, in London, which became his home and his studio for the rest of his life.

Then it occurred to him that if he became a British citizen, the people might accept him more readily. At the age of forty-one, in 1726, "Georg Friedrich Handel" became a British subject. In doing so, he changed his name to George Frideric Handel, which is the spelling that most of his biographers have adopted. In changing his name, he Anglicized his first name, semi-Anglicized his middle name and dropped the umlaut in the last.

Quite unexpectedly the news was circulated that King George I had suffered a stroke and died while riding in his carriage. When the news reached the Prime Minister, Sir Robert Walpole, he leaped on a horse and rode at such speed to Richmond, where the Prince was vacationing, that two horses died under him before he reached the Prince of Wales to inform him of the latter's dramatic change of status.

"I have read my Bible very well."

The coronation of King George II was scheduled at Westminster Abbey for October 11, 1727. Handel was asked to prepare appropriate anthems for the coronation. Although the Archbishops of Canterbury and York wanted to instruct the foreigner Handel on the choice of texts suitable for the occasion, Handel replied, "Do they think that they can write better than prophets and apostles full of the Holy Spirit? I have read my Bible very well and shall choose for myself."

This he did in the use of four Scriptures: 1 Kings 1: 38-40; Psalm 89:14-15; Psalm 21:1 and Psalm 45:1. With these Scripture portions he composed magnificent four-part anthems under significant headings:

"Let Thy Hand Be Strengthened"
"Zadok the Priest"
"The King Shall Rejoice"
"My Heart Is Inditing"

"Zadok the Priest" has been played at every British coronation since.

About ten years later, Handel composed the funeral anthems for Queen Caroline.

Chapter 5

Upon a Solid Foundation

The story of Handel's life in the several years that followed is little more than the story of opera in decline.

The English public was becoming increasingly impatient with the caliber of the artists and entertainment in a language they did not know.

Although in the early eighteenth century an opera performance was also a social occasion, the main interest of the audience lay in the singing more than anything else. However, England was not a "nest of singing birds," and the great singers had to be recruited from the continent, chiefly from Italy.

The imported singers were highly qualified, but they were also eccentric and demanding. It was considered the composer's job to provide music which demonstrated singers' voices to best advantage. Often these singers inserted their own favorite songs, even when they had no relevance to the story. There was much rivalry among the composers and even more among the singers.

In the latter part of 1722, Francesca Cuzzoni arrived to sing for the Royal Academy where Handel was in charge of the music. She was given the leading role in Handel's new opera, *Ottone*, but she refused to sing the great aria composed especially for her, whereupon Handel seized her and threatened to thrust "the shrieking soprano out the open window" until she agreed to sing it. She was not the only eccentric one. Once a castrato tenor threatened to jump on the harpsichord if not allowed his own way. Handel is said to have responded: "Let me know when, and I will advertise it, for more people will come to see you jump than to hear you sing."

All Handel's problems with the singers were in fact a conflict with the opera itself. In a way he was contending against his chosen field of music. In his fondness for opera he was chafing against a trend in England which was irreversible. He toiled long in a sphere too small for him. His long opera drudgery in London was coming to an end. He reigned as absolute monarch in England's music during most of the time he had been there, and no opposition actually drove him from that position. As J. S. Dwight notes in his *Journal of Music*, "It was the ground itself that sank under him. It was Providence itself letting him down upon a solid rock foundation, where he might work with all his own true strengths."

The Beggar's Opera

While Handel was struggling with the serious problem created by the mounting lack of interest in the Italian opera, *The Beggar's Opera* played to packed houses at the Little Theatre in Lincoln's Inn Fields. It was a new kind of a Ballad opera, devised by John Gay and Christopher Pepusch, with music derived from popular English and Scottish tunes, some of which were from Handel himself.

It was a parody of the Italian opera and brilliant satire of the existing society, particularly of the British government under Prime Minister Sir Robert Walpole. The play ran its hilarious course for ninety nights in the early months of 1728. People—rich and poor—flocked to hear it, laughing at its impudent words and humming its familiar tunes.

The success of *The Beggar's Opera* made it clear to Handel that the English public preferred hearing English tunes in English words. Handel had also made the observation that the British public was much better acquainted with the King James English Bible than with Virgil and Homer.

From Opera to Oratorio

In the Italian operas Handel exploited the theatrical intrigues of heathen mythology; now he would draw upon the solid facts of the Bible. His course changed from ethereal myth to solid truth. Sir John Hawkins noted that the sublime sentiments of the Scriptures would best give Handel the opportunity to utilize his greatest talents and would appeal to England's more solid and receptive middle class rather than the fickle ear of the dissipated upper class.

The sleepy church of England, now being aroused by the Wesleyan revival which began in 1739, was more interested in the heroic Bible stories than the trivial poetry of mythology. Handel felt at home in the Bible, and in changing from opera to religious oratorio, his splendid music would no longer suffer by being chained to inferior subject matter.

It is rather disappointing to observe how some biographers of Handel have gone out of their way to point out that in choosing subject matter "from sacred sources Handel was actually impelled more by practical considerations than by exalted motives of religious fervor" (Robert M. Myers). Handel's motives are minutely scrutinized to prove that "nothing in his career warrants the assumption that he was actuated by any motive nobler than desire for monetary reward."

There is no problem here inasmuch as this is generally the motive in any business or profession. There is some suspicion, however, that the biographers subtly may be trying to prepare the reader to approve their interpretations when the subject of the oratorio *Messiah* comes up.

Oratorio is generally regarded as concert music without all the extraneous attraction (or distraction) of scenery, costumes and action. Like opera, an oratorio—religious or secular—portrays certain characters under some particular emotional stress.

The word oratorio has an interesting history. Like the opera, it began in Italy with roots dating back to the sixteenth century. Originally the word meant a prayer hall normally built adjacent to a church, where the meetings were distinct from the regular liturgy. The buildings were rectangular in shape and usually seated between 200 and 400 people. They began to be called the *oratory*, inasmuch as they were erected under the auspices of the Congregation of the Oratory.[1] This was a religious reform movement in the Catholic Church that was founded by Saint Philip Neri (1515-95). The services in the oratory were a means of instruction, and included a message as well as sacred music. Such performances in the oratory were commonly spoken of as oratorios. The use of this term was quickly accepted, not in Rome only, but throughout the whole of Europe.

The first oratorio as such was the *"Rappresentatione di Anima, et di Carpo"* by Emilio de Cavalieri conducted in Rome in 1600. Oratorios of strongly Roman character were soon produced in other Italian cities. These

---

[1] From the Latin *orare*, "to speak or to pray."

were no longer confined to the oratory-style buildings.

Handel first introduced the oratorio to the English people in the period 1732-52. The Handelian oratorio began to be accepted as a result of the vacuum created by London's dissatisfaction with the Italian opera. Following the Peace of Utrecht (1713), concluding the war of the Spanish Succession, English nationalism found strong parallels between itself and the God-favored Israelites of the Old Testament. Consequently, the Handelian historical oratorios based on the biblical stories met with favorable response.

Esther

The idea of an opera in the English language, though urged by Aaron Hill and others, never really caught Handel's interest but the seed sown in his mind concerning an oratorio took almost twenty years to germinate fully.

The performance of his oratorio, *Esther*, on May 2, 1732, marked the beginning of Handel's concert oratorio. On the very first night the crowds were so large that many ticket holders were unable to get inside the Haymarket Theatre. The presence of the royal family enhanced the interest of the public. During the season, *Esther* was performed six times with great applause. Until then an oratorio was completely unknown in England and the Londoners thronged to the theatre, not so much for spiritual edification as for mere curiosity to hear the "novel concoction" of the revered Mr. Handel.

Despite the success of *Esther*, Handel was not fully convinced as to the musical potential of oratorio. In 1739 Handel composed music for Gay's *"Ode for St. Cecelia's Day."* In 1740, Charles Jennens sent Handel a new libretto which was an adaptation of Milton's poems *"L'Allegro"* (the cheerful man) and *"Il Penserosa"* (the pensive man) with some additions of his own.

Though the poems were non-dramatic, Handel provided fresh, lively music. These were appreciated at least by the English middle class; however, nothing seemed to attract full houses.

Handel was frustrated, discouraged and suffered severe financial losses. On top of all else, the strain of these years took their toll and he suffered a severe stroke which paralyzed his right arm and brought mental disorder. He was prevailed upon to go to the famous spa of Aachen (Aix-la-Chapelle). With Handel's typical determination the recovery was so rapid and so complete that the nuns in attendance claimed a sure miracle had occurred.

Handel returned to England and renewed his efforts at opera, from which he had not been fully cured. The people seemed to realize that Handel was more than just another ordinary composer. They began to treat him with the kind of respect that his genius deserved.

One particular sign of recognition was the erection of a statue of him at Vauxhall, the famous public garden by the river Thames where rich and poor, young and old alike, came to enjoy themselves in a variety of ways. The statue was carved by the distinguished French sculptor Louis-Francois Roubiliac "out of one entire block of white marble" and was given a place of honor "in a grand niche" erected on purpose and set by various greens which formed, in miniature, a sort of woody theatre. Sir John Hawkins praised it highly because the artist caught something of the mixture of ease and alertness which are so essentially that of the great composer.

The statue is today in view at the Victoria and Albert Museum in London.

Chapter 6

Birth of the Oratorio Messiah

The vision for biblical oratorio was developing in Handel's mind for fifteen or twenty years before it became a reality.

In his *History of Music*, Charles Burney (1726-1814), who first knew Handel when Burney was a boy, quotes from a letter that Aaron Hill, a collaborator of Handel, had written to Handel as early as 1732: "I cannot forbear to tell you the earnestness of my wishes, that, as you have made such considerable steps towards it, already, you would let us owe to your inimitable genius, the establishment of *musick*, upon a foundation of good poetry; where the excellence of the *sound* should no longer be dishonoured, by the poorness of the *sense* it is chained to. My meaning is, that you would be resolute enough, to deliver us from our *Italian bondage*; and demonstrate, that *English* is soft enough for opera, when composed by poets, who know how to distinguish the sweetness of our Tongue, from the *strength* of it, where the latter is less necessary."

Despite such compelling requests which urged Handel to write opera which would be based on substantial words and in the English language, in 1741, Handel made his last attempt at returning to opera, his first love. The curtain came down on February 10, 1741, and Handel's operatic career came to a close. It was another two centuries before a Handel opera was again seen on the London stage.

Handel's first efforts at oratorio were made in Italy in 1707-08 when he composed *La Resurrezione*, using material from the Bible, and *Il Trionfo* . . . which was purely allegorical.

Esther, a revision of his earlier work, *Haman and Mordeca*, came in 1732. The music here was after the manner of a coronation service. *Deborah* was written in 1733. Handel's more mature, heroic-style compositions—*Saul* and *Israel in Egypt*—were produced in 1738. Here the better developed anthem-like choruses began to appear. In the text, the superintendency and faithfulness of God to His people was clearly evident. Handel had attained a higher flexibility in his choral writing. The foundations were being laid for developing a form in which the chorus was the central factor. This led to the splendid oratorios of his manhood.

While Handel sat in his home on Brook Street brooding over his future, on Saturday, August 22, 1741, Charles Jennens brought a folder to his house. He said, "Here is a collection called *Messiah*. See what you can make of it."

After Jennens left, Handel at once began reading the text. He saw that the words were all taken from the Scriptures, including portions from Job, Psalms, Isaiah, Lamentations, Haggai, Zechariah, Malachi, Matthew, Luke, John, Romans, 1st Corinthians, Hebrews and Revelation. He at once must have been impressed by the sequence in which the Scriptures were arranged.

Contrary to the report of biographers generally, Handel did *not* begin writing the music at once. That would have been quite impossible.

An example of the problem involved is taken from the experience of a Bible expositor. Alexander Maclaren (1826-1910), a distinguished pastor in England, acquired the reputation as "prince of expository preachers." His sixteen-volume commentary on the whole Bible is still being printed and highly acclaimed.

Dr. Maclaren was known to have devoted as many as sixty hours in the preparation of a single expository message.

There was Handel, faced with the enormous task of writing music—most appropriate music—for the exalted Scriptures which reveal God's drama of redemption in and through His only begotten Son, the Lord Jesus Christ. How would this man begin writing suitable music for the greatest subject in the universe?

It is at once apparent that he had to spend many hours in studying and understanding the full meaning of those seventy-nine Bible verses. If it took Maclaren sixty hours to prepare one gospel message, how much time—how many days—did Handel spend in grasping the essential meaning of the divine truth concerning the glorious Redeemer?

It may have come to him as a fresh revelation to see how the mediatorial work of Christ was so minutely foretold in the Old Testament Scriptures, and then, so plenarily fulfilled in His life and work as recorded by the inspired New Testament writers. The resplendent realization of prophecy fulfilled never fails to strengthen a person's faith in God and leaves no doubt as to the inerrancy of the holy Scriptures. Handel had to understand what those Scriptures meant in their context. He had to comprehend also the meaning of the difficult passages in 1 Corinthians and Revelation in order to grasp the great truth in God's grand finale, which he communicated with consummate excellence in his *Hallelujah* chorus, in his *Worthy* outburst and in his unending *Amen.*

Handel saw that the Scriptures before him were not mere biographical facts concerning the life and work of Christ. He perceived that Christ's earthly life takes on its full royal grandeur when set against the vast background of fulfilled prophecy. The Scriptures in the oratorio *Messiah* chronicle the grand redemption epic where human destiny was inextricably dependent upon the mediatorial work of the Redeemer through whom the divine symphony was forever perfected.

Like the psalmist of old, Handel might very well have said, "While I was musing, the fire burned, then spake I with my tongue." Or to borrow a line from his approving contemporary, the poet Alexander Pope, there sat the famous composer "with fire in each eye and papers in each hand," or with papers in one hand while the other hand was on the keys of his harpsichord. Many of the first papers probably found their way to the waste basket, but he persevered and remained secluded in his study for those twenty-four days.

Handel became completely immersed in his subject. He seemed to forget all the world around him. Food brought to him at regular intervals was often untouched, and the servant would see the enraptured composer praying, sobbing or just staring into space. On another occasion when he was composing the *Hallelujah Chorus* the servant stood in silent astonishment to see his master's tears drop on his page and make ink blotches as he penned his notes. While he was composing "He was despised," a visitor found the trembling composer sobbing with intense emotion. "Whether I was in my body or out of my body as I wrote *Messiah*," Handel said later. "I know not."

It becomes apparent that in writing *Messiah* Handel was deeply stirred and conspicuously unctioned by God.

Thomas Carlyle (1795-1881) said that "music was the speech of angels." Charles Kingsley (1819-1875), English novelist, expanded Carlyle's remark: "Music has been called the speech of angels. I will go a step further and call it the speech of God Himself. Without words, it is wonderful, blessed; one of God's gifts to men, but in singing you have both wonders together —music and words." A further word of illumination concerning music comes from J. G. Brainard: "God is its author, and not man; He laid the key-note of all harmonies; He planned all perfect combinations, and He made us so that we could hear and understand."

Meditating on the divine words of Scripture, Handel's soul was ignited from above as he wrote his immortal composition in accents and harmonies which seemed to exceed his capabilities. It is good that he left a few statements concerning all that went on during those twenty-four wonderful days. He said, "I thought I saw all heaven open before me and the great God Himself." This is a most revealing assertion and must not be taken lightly or just totally disregarded, as is often the case.

His intense remark is very similar to the expression of Franz Joseph Haydn (1732-1809), who was incalculably influenced by Handel's *Messiah* in writing his great oratorio *Creation*.

In 1808, just a year before his death, a grand performance of *Creation* took place in Vienna. The composer himself was there for the occasion. Old and feeble, he was brought into the great hall in a wheelchair. His presence caused an electrifying enthusiasm among all. As the orchestra and chorus burst forth with full power in the passage, "And there was light," a crescendo of unrestrained applause broke out.

Moved by this response, the godly musician struggled to his feet. Summoning all his strength, he raised his trembling arms, and cried, "No, No! Not from me, but from thence—from heaven above comes all!" Although he fell back in his chair and had to be carried from the hall, the old master had made his point in a dramatic and unforgettable manner.

One can hardly dispute the fact that this is precisely what Handel intended to convey when he said he saw "all heaven" and "the great God Himself."

Biographers of Handel through the centuries since then have hardly known how to interpret these remarks of the composer. For the most part, they seem to minimize their significance and simply attribute the greatness of *Messiah* to the genius of the composer. This is understandable because the natural man does not comprehend the meaning, the power and the greatness of the Word of God.

Handel completed *Messiah* in less than twenty-four uninterrupted days. In that time, he created the full musical notes on 265 pages of manuscript. When he finished the composition, he placed it in a drawer, where it remained for seven weeks.

The Contribution of Charles Jennens

Although Charles Jennens is generally dismissed lightly by biographers, he was one of the most influential people in the life of Handel. He was fifteen years younger than Handel. Like Handel, he was heavy, and a bachelor, but whereas he "spent money; Handel saved it." Jennens inherited great wealth, and spent his time mixing with writers, composers and painters. He also tried writing some Latin poetry. He spent money lavishly on himself and enjoyed the pomp and showmanship which money can procure. He travelled in a magnificent surrey drawn by four horses with plumes, and attended by four lackeys.

His ventures in tampering with the works of Shakespeare, brought down upon him the wrath of the learned Dr. Samuel Johnson, who nicknamed him "Solyman the Magnificent."

Nevertheless, he was a highly intelligent man and was always ready with words of wisdom, "and if what he said was not in the Bible, it always sounded as if it should have been" (Paul Henry Lang).

In compiling the Scriptures for the *Messiah*, Jennens began with Old Testament prophecies. Then he took the New Testament accounts which validated those predictions. The Scriptures which Jennens used in his libretto (text) were all taken from the familiar King James Version except those from the Psalms, where an older version found in the Anglican Book of Common Prayer was followed. The Scripture text was unaltered except in a few instances where it was slightly shortened.

Jennens was rather impressed with his own abilities and often urged Handel to make certain revisions in his compositions, including *Messiah*. Handel valued the friendship and encouragement of Jennens and for the most part he just shrugged off the suggestions for the revision of his music.

Biographers observe correctly that Jennens had a subtle purpose behind his selection of the Scripture texts. The passages he chose presented the truth concerning redemption from sin, including the resurrection, at a time when Anglicans of the orthodox caste found themselves in theological conflict with Deists and Freethinkers.

Jennens recognized the value of words and content in musical compositions. It was he who first suggested to Handel the use of Milton's verse from some of his shorter compositions like *"Il Penseroso."* He perceived that in order for a musical composition to be substantial it required substantial words. It was because of this persuasion that he presented to Handel the masterly arrangement from the Scriptures which constitutes the *Messiah.* What he created exists as a work of art in itself and for this reason the name of Jennens lives on with the immortal *Messiah.*

Few writers take cognizance of the vision that Jennens had when he organized the Scriptures for *Messiah.* The theme he intended was "Mystery of Godliness," which is expounded in one verse of Scripture from the apostle Paul's first letter to Timothy: "And without controversy great is the mystery of godliness: God was manifest in the flesh, justified in the Spirit, seen of angels, preached among the Gentiles, believed on in the world, received up into glory." This verse is often printed at the top of the *Messiah* libretto with no explanation. Another word from Paul which Jennens referred to is the verse in Colossians where it is stated that in the Redeemer "are hid all the treasures of wisdom and knowledge."

Messiah—A Work of Art

Handel's *Messiah* was born of failure and affliction. Though he was deeply discouraged, he arose courageously to create the masterpiece which has delighted and consoled the English world for some two hundred and fifty years.

After thirty years of unremitting toil, Handel undertook to compose what became his musical masterpiece. There were imperishable songs scattered

Handel's home, studios and servant quarters
at 57 Lower Brook Street, London - (the big black dot)

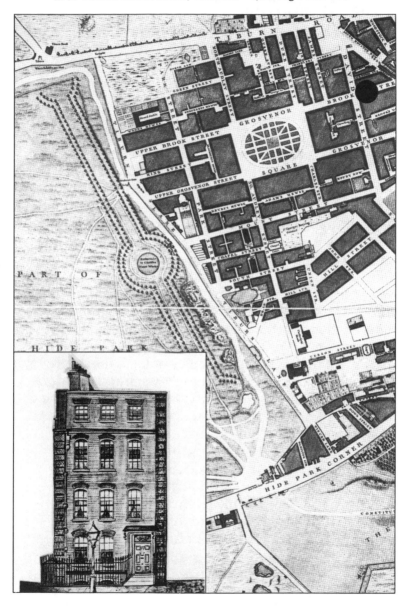

through operas and his other compositions. Now they would be utilized in the supreme achievement of the man who was God's finely-tuned instrument. George Eliot (Mary Ann Evans, 1819-80), novelist, adds the appropriate word: " 'Tis God gives the skill, but not without men's hands: He could not make Antonio Stradivari's violins without Antonio."

Handel knew his Bible well and was particularly fond of the prophets and the epistles of the apostle Paul. He was deeply impressed with what was to him the one pervading theme of the Scriptures—the fall and the redemption of man. Now he drew from all the resources of his creativity in making an eloquent exposition of his faith through appropriate music.

In this unique effort, he drew from the pristine fount of divine inspiration, from the holy Scriptures themselves. Perhaps this is why men are bewildered by its strange power. At the age of fifty-six Handel composed the work which is the fullest expression of his soul, possibly the highest product of musical art— the *Messiah*. It is not so much the kind of music as it is the soul of the music itself. Music in its highest sphere is the expression of the believer's worship and adoration of the Redeemer. In such worship the redeemed soul glimpses the reality of heaven, as John Milton so well descanted:

There let the pealing organ blow,
To the full voiced choir below,
In service high, and anthems clear,
As may with sweetness, through mine ear,
Dissolve me into ecstasies,
And bring all heaven before mine eyes.

Some observers state quite unequivocally that there will never again be written a composition equal to the transcendent achievement of Handel's *Messiah*. Dean Edward Ramsay expressed that feeling: "We cannot conceive the possibility of any human composition permanently taking the place of the *Messiah*. The more high music is cultivated, the more marked amongst great composers is the supremacy of Handel."

The use of the Bible in English proved helpful. While the prose of the King James translation has no metrical structure as such, it does, nevertheless, have a controlled rhetorical rhythm. Measured sentences are frequently divided into balanced clauses by a colon or a semi-colon.

There is no impersonation of dramatic characters but simply a contemplation of the Scriptures which delineate what God was achieving through the great Redeemer.

In turning from the opera to the oratorio, Handel did not entirely forsake his fundamental passion for dramatic music but merely relinquished its theatrical aspects.

With his long experience in opera, he developed a keen sense for stunning dramatic situations and whenever his theme afforded him opportunity in this respect, he invariably responded with suitable musical garnish.

Sir Thomas Beecham, a devotee of Handel's *Messiah* and his other oratorios, noted in his memoirs, as quoted by Jacobi: "Since his time, mankind has heard no music written for voices which can even feebly rival his for grandeur of build and tone, nobility and tenderness of melody, scholastic skill in ingenuity and inexhaustible variety of effect."

Dean Ramsay gives three specific reasons why Handel's music in the *Messiah* towers above all other musical productions. First, "the majesty and sublimity with which Handel treats his subject. Second, his great powers in expressing pathos; and third, the exquisite appropriateness of the music to the words at hand."

This simple appraisal commends itself as being suitable. However, it must at once be stated additionally that the distinctiveness of the oratorio is not only the music but the words as well—they are God-given Words. In the *Messiah* we have God's excellent, inerrant Words expressed in the most celebrated music. These two wonders, so felicitously united, constitute the amplitude and the power of *Messiah*.

Handel's power of expressing the leading thought of the text before him in musical language is remarkable. He seizes the meaning of the words and expresses it in his musical notes in a way whereby the listener perceives the music to belong inseparably—exclusively—to those words and that it could not be used for any other words. It goes without saying that Handel had to understand the words clearly in order to create such appropriate music!

Handel became blind in 1753. R. A. Streatfeild tells about the performance of Handel's oratorio, *Samson* which was composed right after his composition of *Messiah*. Handel, by then blind, was present. The audience was strangely moved when Mr. Beard sang with great feeling the famous *air, Total Eclipse*: "No sun, no moon! All dark amid the blaze of noon."

At the age of fifty-six, Handel completed *Messiah* —his *Magnum Opus*—in less than four weeks. The poet Keats died in his twenty-sixth year; Shelley drowned before he was thirty; among the music composers Schubert died at thirty-one; Mozart at thirty-five; and Mendelssohn at thirty-eight. Handel is best known for works composed after his first half century.

The distinction due to Shakespeare in the art of poetry, to Michelangelo in sculpture and painting, belongs justly to Handel in the majesty of music.

On September 14, 1741, he brought the final chorus for *Messiah* to a triumphant close with the signature SDG, Latin for *Soli Deo Gloria* (to God alone the glory).

Chapter 7

First Performance of Messiah

Though it is often assumed that London was the site of the first performance of *Messiah*, Dublin rightly claims this distinction.

In the autumn of 1741, Handel received an invitation from the Lord-Lieutenant of Ireland and the Governors of three charitable institutions in Dublin to come there. Handel had made some plans to return to Germany, but he accepted the invitation immediately. A new enthusiasm began to surge through him.

Gathering the principal singers was no small task. The choirs of two cathedrals had been trained for two weeks, and great enthusiasm was mounting. The first performance of Handel's Grand Oratorio was scheduled for April 13, 1742. Because the music hall seated only seven hundred, the people were advised by the Dublin papers to come "without swords and hoops."

Finally came the night for the first performance of *Messiah*. The music hall proved far too small. Hundreds stood on the street. The oratorio was performed excellently and brought satisfaction to all present. The performance was repeated at the same place on May 13th, and the newspapers reported generously:

> On Tuesday last, Mr. Handel's Sacred Grand Oratorio, *Messiah*, was performed in the Neal's Music Hall in Fishamble-street; the best judges allowed it to be the most finished piece of music. Words are wanting to express the exquisite delight it afforded to the admiring crowded audience. The sublime, the grand and the tender, adapted to the most elevated, majestic and moving words, conspired to transport and charm the ravished heart and ear.
>
> It is but justice to Mr. Handel that the world should know he generously gave the money arising from the grand performance, to be equally shared by the Society for Relieving Prisoners, the Charitable Infirmary and Mercer's Hospital, for which they will ever gratefully remember his name . . .

From Dublin, Benjamin Victor wrote to the Reverend William Rothery: "You must be a lover of music—if Handel's *Messiah* should be performed in London... I beg it as a favour to me, that you will go early, and take your wife with you, your time and money cannot be so well employed; take care to get a book of the oratorio some days before, that you may well digest the subject, there you will hear *glad tidings* and truly divine rejoicing at the birth of *Christ*, and feel real sorrows for His sufferings . . . As much as I detest fatigue and inconvenience, I would ride forty miles in the wind and rain to be present at a performance of the *Messiah* in London, under the conduct of Handel—I remember it there—he had an hundred instruments, and fifty voices! O how magnificent the full choruses."

In view of *Messiah's* subsequent poor reception in London, it is noteworthy that no word of criticism is known to have been uttered concerning the propriety of the musical or the place of its performance.

The Encouragement of Susanna Cibber

The production of *Messiah* was built around the soft contralto voice of Susanna Cibber. She was a lovely, dark-haired woman who had gained recognition as probably the outstanding actress in London, especially when she took the part of Polly in *Beggar's Opera*. Handel had known her since she was a child. She already knew the music of *Messiah* probably as well as the composer because he had played it for her on many occasions.

She had an unhappy life, losing two children in infancy and coping with a husband who was a drunkard. Perhaps because her own life had been marked by much sorrow and tragedy, she not only understood Handel's music, but she could more readily identify with him in his trials and struggles for acceptance.

Susanna's voice, though not very strong, was probably unsurpassed in sweetness and depth of feeling by any singer in England. People called her "the Nightingale," and it is not far-fetched to speak of her as the "brokenhearted Nightingale." She could effectively convey Handel's music to the audience because she did it with such personal emotion.

When she intoned with her whole heart and intense voice the words, *"He was despised and rejected of men,"* it is recorded that the ladies present dabbed tears from their eyes, and that Swift's friend, Dr. Patrick Delaney, a prominent clergyman, who was seated in one of the boxes, exclaimed, "Woman, for this be all thy sins forgiven thee."

"The most finished piece of music," the Dublin papers reported, and there is little doubt that it was the "Nightingale's" voice that evoked the further comment, it "transported and charmed the ravished heart and ear."

Handel was very fond of Susanna Cibber and their relationship "matured into a great and clean friendship," as even his severest critics grudgingly admitted. She shared his sorrows and encouraged him not to give up hope. The Dublin success had made him forget how poorly London had treated him, but when he returned to his old home he was again reminded of that coldness and lack of acceptance that existed in England. It was Susanna's enthusiasm as much as anything else that helped Handel to decide on the performance of *Messiah* in London.

There was a great deal of favorable comment from different sources in Dublin, including some verse by Mr. Al White:

> None but the great Messiah could inflame
> And raise his soul to so sublime a theme
> Profound the thoughts, the subject all divine.
> . . . .
> In Him were all their Prophecies complete.
> The Word made flesh, both God and man became,
>
> Then let all nations glorify His name!
> Let hallelujahs round the globe be sung,
> To our Messiah, from a virgin sprung.

After another performance or two, Handel returned to London.

Chapter 8

Performance of Messiah in London

The first performance of *Messiah* in London was set for March 19, 1743 at Covent Garden. Even though it was not announced by name, but as a new, sacred oratorio, the religious authorities at once raised the objection that the performance of the life of Christ in a playhouse was sacrilegious.

It was stated rather explicitly by Philalethes in a letter to the *Universal Spectator*: "The oratorio either is an act of religion or it is not; if it is: I ask if the play-house is a fit temple to perform it in, or a company of players fit ministers of God's Word, for in that case such they are made."

It should be stated that no cathedral or church was made available for this purpose and the only other alternative for Handel was to have it in a theatre. The opposition did its very best to prevent the perform-ance, but since King George II had announced his intention to attend, it could not be cancelled very gracefully.

As Handel began to play, the people listened in awe; when the triumphant Hallelujah Chorus, which declares that Christ would come and reign forever as King of kings and Lord of lords, the people were greatly moved. King George II was so deeply stirred with the exalted music that he rose to his feet and remained standing until the last echo of the thunderous chorus had ended.

Whether the King did it because he was genuinely moved or because he felt some obligation to compensate for the apathy of his subjects is not certain. Be that as it may, many biographers believe that it was he who initiated the custom of standing when the Hallelujah Chorus comes on.

Handel's enemies kept up their protest and called the performance irreligious. Others called it dull. Most Londoners simply stayed away. Despite the King's presence, *Messiah* was a failure in London and after three performances Handel withdrew his sacred oratorio amid a storm of disapproval.

Handel's achievement rises to the same high level as Milton's *Paradise Lost*. Like Milton, Handel's greatest powers were exercised in sacred song. Like Milton, he rises to the highest point of grandeur and majesty when engaged in expressing the worship of the great Redeemer. It is, therefore, a little incredible that Milton's *Paradise Lost* and Handel's *Messiah*—the two most sublime works on sacred subjects in the course of centuries—should have been received unfavorably when first presented to the English people. The tenor of the times at least partially explains the apparent indifference.

After 1743, *Messiah* was not heard in London again until the Spring of 1745, when it was twice performed at Covent Garden before the unresponsive audiences.

The London Daily Post best responds to the critics:

"The theatre on this occasion ought to be entered into with more solemnity than a church; inasmuch as entertainment you go to is really in itself the noblest adoration and homage paid to the Deity that ever was done in one. So sublime an act of devotion as this representation carries in it, the heart and ear duly tuned to it would consecrate even hell itself—it is the action that is done in it that hallows the place and not the place the action."

Exactly so!

"It is the action that is done in it that hallows the place and not the place the action." When two or three believers meet in the name of the Lord, He is in their midst. They become oblivious to place. They know neither theatre nor cathedral. They are enthralled with the Lord.

Acclaim

Amidst the varied circumstances, Handel's creativity never ceased. Having founded the new style of musical compositions, he went right on composing oratorios. Many of them were built around the special voice of his "Nightingale," Susanna Cibber.

Although the response of Londoners as a whole was slow in coming, the great thinkers of the day acclaimed him as "the greatest genius in music that has ever trodden the soil of England." Apart from Addison, who held a personal grudge against Handel, the recognition came from such men as Pope, Hogarth, Fielding and others.

Of all composers, Handel knew best how to achieve grand effects with simple means. Bach, who was born the same year as Handel in the same corner of Germany, admired his great achievements, and died in 1750 without having met him personally.

Haydn, of Austrian birth, whose own oratorios were modelled on those of Handel, simply called Handel, "the master of us all."

Chapter 9

"It Will Rise Again"

Handel, still shunning the daylight after his failures, one night met William Hogarth, the famous artist, at Rose Coffee House, where the artist spent many hours sketching the picturesque life of the streets. The two had much in common. As a youngster, Hogarth too had to fight against the will of a stern father, who wanted his son William to be a printer like he was.

As they reminisced, they could look out and see the Covent Garden where Handel's *Messiah* was temporarily buried.

"Someday," said Hogarth with conviction, "it will rise again."

Handel was dejected and felt burdened because of his financial misfortunes, and the fellowship with his good friend was stimulating. Their visit continued long into the night, and they could hardly believe it when they saw the glow of dawn brightening the eastern sky.

In those early morning hours small herds of sheep passed the coffee shop on their way to the nearby market. William Hogarth loved sheep and Handel remembered the shepherds with unshorn locks at Calabria near Rome where they sang their Christmas carols. Handel started humming a tune from the *Messiah*: "He shall feed His flock like a shepherd and He shall gather the lambs with His arm and carry them in His bosom."

Suddenly they were interrupted by a familiar voice. It was Captain Thomas Coram, founder and director of the highly respected Foundling Hospital of London. Hogarth introduced them, and the Foundling Hospital (home for deserted children) quickly became the subject of their conversation.

Handel hummed a tune or two from *Messiah* for the benefit of the Captain and reportedly said to him right there and then, "How would you like me to give a concert with instrumental music for your children?"

Captain Coram immediately accepted the offer. Soon thereafter Handel met with the Foundling Hospital Committee and was enrolled as governor of the Hospital, even as his friend Hogarth had been. Handel bought a small organ for the new chapel at the children's home and showed them how to use it and care for it.

The Foundling Hospital

The Foundling Hospital was opened in 1739 for the reception and care of deserted young children. From its very beginning this highly respected charity was entirely free and all foundlings were admitted without exception. Any person bringing a child to the place rang a bell at the gate, deposited the foundling in a basket hung at the inner door and then waited to find out whether the infant was accepted at once or not. No questions whatever were asked about the child's parentage or background. When the full quota of children had been admitted, a notice was placed at the door stating, "The house is full."

Susanna Cibber, alto in *Messiah* and close friend of the composer

Inside of the Chapel at the Foundling Hospital

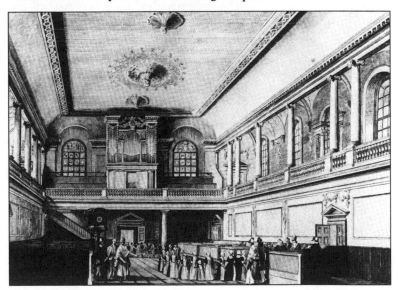

The performance of *Messiah* was set for May 1, 1750, at the Foundling Hospital's new chapel. The boys in the place made up the chorus, and Mr. Handel himself met with them at least once a week for a whole year to train them. They loved him and looked up to him with adoring admiration. He fully reciprocated their affection and told them on numerous occasions, "You are my family!" The solos were assigned to adult professionals, which, of course included Susanna Cibber.

The day for the performance was fast approaching. Handel composed a special anthem for the children called, *"The Foundling Anthem,"* and Ned, a bright boy of eleven, would be playing it for all the guests at the banquet following the performance of *Messiah*. The distinguished guests at the banquet would include the Prince and Princess of Wales.

The Unforgettable Day

There was great excitement as the children were preparing. First they had to "lay" the tables for the banquet in the East wing. All was finally completed to the satisfaction of the supervisor.

Carriages in great numbers were already arriving, including the magnificent coach of Charles Jennens, drawn by four plumed horses. There was a great deal of confusion. Apparently more tickets were sold than the capacity of the chapel. People were pushing and shouting. Order was finally restored when it was announced that there would be another performance on May 15th and all the tickets would be honored.

"Here he comes!" Ned shouted and hurried to be the first to greet the Master. Then a lovely lady, Susanna Cibber, arrived. "This I have brought for you," she said, and handed Handel a bouquet of flowers. "And this is for you," she added, and handed Rose, a leader among the girls, a big box of sweets.

The clock began striking twelve and Handel, followed by Ned and the other choir boys, entered the chapel. Though they were not to sing in the choir, the girls, dressed in their Sunday-best uniforms, also entered, following Rose to their seats opposite the boys. The Prince and Princess of Wales and their court were seated exactly at twelve. Twelve hundred people crowded into the chapel.

Handel opened the organ he had purchased for the children, and soon the overture of his *Messiah* rang out and echoed magnificently from the arches of the chapel, as if the music came from above.

Place and time seemed to vanish as a tenor voice, as if calling from above, began singing "Comfort ye, comfort ye My people..." "Every valley shall be exalted," and here Ned knew that the chorus was to begin.

"And the glory of the Lord shall be revealed," rang out sweetly from the choir led by Ned, "and all flesh shall see it together, for the mouth of the Lord hath spoken it."

The chapel was filled with heavenly sound and strangely attentive hearts. Susanna sang in her sweet melting voice, "He shall feed His flock like a shepherd: and He shall gather the lambs with His arm, and carry them in His bosom . . ." The audience was strangely affected since they could not help but notice affectionately all those dear young children abandoned by parents, and understand how gently the good Shepherd had led them and how graciously He had provided for them.

Again, as Susanna began singing, "He was despised and rejected of men...", hearts were deeply touched. The organ "sobbed" as the boys' choir joined in, "Surely He hath borne our griefs and carried our sorrows . . ."

Waves of resplendent light poured through the

stained-glass windows of the chapel; wave after wave of glorious sound surged throughout the spacious room, and the gates of heaven seemed very close . . . as the chorus of children rang out with such joy and gladness:

Hallelujah, for the Lord God omnipotent reigneth . . .
   King of kings, and Lord of lords: Hallelujah.

Suddenly, the Prince of Wales rose from his seat, the Princess also, and the whole audience as well—as if prompted by a superior power—rose to its feet in recognition of the genius of Handel and—much more than that—bowed in sincere worship of the great Redeemer.

Captain Coram, the founder of the Hospital and William Hogarth, who helped in those unique ways, must have been gratified and felt amply rewarded.

Messiah at last began to conquer the Londoners, both small and great!

After these first performances, a Mrs. Ann Granville Dewes wrote her brother, as follows:

> I hope you find Mr. Handel well. His wonderful *Messiah* will never be out of my head. I may say my heart was raised almost to heaven by it. It is only those people who have not felt the leisure of devotion that can make any objection to that performance which is calculated to raise our devotion and to make us truly sensible of the divine Words.

A few years later Miss Catherine Talbot wrote:

> The only public place I have been this winter, was last Friday, to hear the *Messiah*. I think it is impossible for the most trifling not to be the better for it. I was wishing all the Jews, Heathens, and Infidels in the world (a pretty full house you'll say) to be present.

Without minimizing in the slightest the great contribution of Susanna Cibber and the other trained participants, it is noteworthy that it was the chorus which rang out from the melodious hearts of those deserted youngsters that first really awakened England to the greatness and power of *Messiah*.

The net income from the performance totalled seven hundred pounds, and every penny was placed into the Hospital fund.

At the banquet that followed the performance, the Prince of Wales, who would become King George III, called the oratorio a "divine" work, adding a special observation about the words: "Without that unique compilation from the Bible," he said, "the true revelation of *Messiah* could not be achieved."

Exactly so!

It is well to remember what the Prince had to say about the *words* of the oratorio!

Two weeks later, *Messiah* was performed again before another twelve hundred people packed inside the chapel. The proceeds from the performance again went for the work in behalf of those poor children.

Thereafter *Messiah* was performed at the Foundling Hospital chapel every year, with ever increasing enthusiasm. The composition, which for seven or eight years had endured the apathy and scorn of indifference, suddenly became England's favorite musical.

Chapter 10

Messiah:
Entertainment or Edification?

As Handel's one hundredth birthday anniversary was approaching, a centennial celebration at Westminster Abbey was announced for May 29th, 1784. Elaborate plans were made for the performance of Handel's "sublime oratorio," the *Messiah.*

The interior of the Abbey was remodelled for the special occasion, including the erection of "a large new organ." The number of instruments and voices was greatly increased. Many of the performers came from remote parts of the kingdom at their own expense.

Early in the morning of the special day, a large number of persons of all ranks began to arrive, though the doors would not be opened until nine o'clock. The immense space was crowded to overflowing, in number more than four thousand. When the royal family arrived shortly after twelve, the performance began.

The celebration was "executed in a manner worthy of the great composer," the *European Magazine* reported, and stated further that "when the whole chorus from each side of the orchestra, joined by all the instruments, burst out, *He is the King of glory,"* the effect was noticeably overwhelming, judging from "the plenitude of satisfaction which appeared in the countenances" of performers and guests alike.

Miss Mary Hamilton, seated with Sir Joshua Reynolds and Dr. Burney, noted in her diary, "I was so delighted that I thought myself in the heavenly regions. The harmony was so unbroken that it was like the fall of waters from one source, imperceptibly blended. The spectacle too was sublime. So universal a silence. So great a number of people . . ."

John Newton (1725-1807)

From the very beginning, some of the Anglican clergy objected to all *playhouse* performances as a kind of profanation, while others with equal zeal opposed all *cathedral* performances of the oratorio as sacrilegious.

The highly esteemed John Newton, author of "Amazing Grace" and other great hymns, undertook to set things straight by preaching fifty "expository discourses," as he called them, on the Scriptures which form the oratorio *Messiah*. He was pastor of the large Anglican congregation at the Parish Church of St. Mary Woolnoth, and regarded generally as a leading evangelical.

Strictly speaking, his discourses were not primarily of an "expository" nature, but they are fine gospel messages. He preached them on fifty successive Sundays in 1784 and 1785. There was a general feeling that in taking up so popular a theme, Mr. Newton was making use of the current interest in order to attract attention to his own work.

Mr. Newton definitely approved the selection and the sequence of the Scriptures in the *Messiah*. Nowhere did he speak unkindly about Mr. Handel, and he regarded the musical composition as being "executed in a masterly manner." He did, however, express some disapproval.

In his first sermon, he complained that the vast majority of the performers and the people who attended the performance were incapable "of entering into the spirit of the subject."

In his fourth discourse, Mr. Newton looked at the *Messiah* and its adherents in a very severe manner. "I represent to myself," he said, "a number of persons of various characters, involved in one common charge of high treason. They are already in a state of confinement, but not yet brought to their trial... They choose to make the solemnities of their impending trial, the character of their judge, and the awful sentence to which they are exposed, the groundwork of a musical entertainment... The King, out of His great clemency and compassion, sends them a gracious message . . . with a free and a full pardon . . . Instead of taking a single step towards a compliance with His goodness, they set His message likewise to music, and this together with a description of their present state and of the fearful doom awaiting them if they continue obstinate, is sung for their diversion, accompanied by many instruments."

It must at once be conceded that what Mr. Newton said was no doubt true of *some* of the people who attended the oratorio, but he missed the mark when he failed to perceive that this was by no means true of all who listened to the words and music of the *Messiah*.

Obviously, this was not the "finest hour" of England's great evangelical leader. How did the people sitting there and listening to such reproach feel about it? Surely there were some there who came because their interest in the truth of redemption had been aroused by hearing the musical composition.

Would such criticism inspire them to come back for "spiritual edification," or would it simply add to their confusion and create indifference to the pulpit rhetoric?

"The same great truths," he continued, "divested of the music, when delivered from the pulpit, are heard by many admirers of the oratorio with indifference, too often with contempt." It is unfortunate that Mr. Newton felt that he was in a position to judge the hearts of the performers and know the motives of the audience.

Sermon number thirty six, which covers the text of the Hallelujah Chorus, carried further censure: "However great the power of music... it cannot soften and change the hard heart, it cannot bend the obdurate will of man. If all the people who successively hear the *Messiah*, who are struck and astonished for the moment, by this chorus in particular, were to bring away with them an abiding sense of the importance of the sentiment it contains, the nation would soon wear a new face."

This is incorrect! It tends to imply that all those who hear a great sermon come away with an *abiding* and *visible* sense of its spiritual importance, and this is not the case. Mr. Newton looked on the dark side of how people respond to the ministry of music.

The Wesleys

Whereas Newton considered every form of music, except the simple, unpretentious hymn singing, as belonging exclusively to the domain of Satan, the families of John and Charles Wesley, highly gifted in music, did not think it profitable to leave all the best melodies to the devil.

John Wesley, in August 1758, heard *Messiah* at Bristol. "I doubt if that congregation was ever so serious at a sermon," he wrote, "as they were during this performance. In many parts, especially several of the choruses, it exceeded my expectation."

The increasing acceptance of *Messiah* throughout England coincides with the Wesleys' revival that swept Great Britain with a strong wave of Christian fervor and zeal. Handel's *Messiah* gave musical expression to the very doctrines of redemption which Wesley and Whitfield rescued from long neglect in England's sleepy church. No student of history fails to observe how England's unparalleled evangelical revival was linked and enhanced by the strong presentation of the Redeemer in Handel's *Messiah*.

Handel's *Messiah* began to be closely identified with nationalistic feelings. It was indeed better to support such a movement, and emphasize the full spiritual character and power of which it is capable, than to make the ill-advised effort of running it down as something evil. Robert Hall, an eloquent English nonconformist, refused to share Newton's objections, but testified how deeply he was affected by the great celebration at the Abbey in 1784. It impressed him as "a great act of national assent to the fundamental truths of the [Christian] religion."

Handel's *Messiah* and the evangelical revival went hand in hand and deeply influenced the people of England so that they did indeed "wear a new face," which Mr. Newton apparently failed to see.

Who is there that will look at England's history and fail to see that these influences were part of a very strong force which kept England from a frightful revolution such as swept France in 1789?

In his closing discourse Newton rehearsed his objections to the *Messiah*. One was "the great impropriety of making the fundamental truths of Christianity the theme of public amusement." Another, which he frequently repeated, was that "the great truths of God" were not enhanced by Handel's music, but that they were buried beneath its "impressive grandeur."

It is to be regretted that John Newton, according to the nature of his remarks, never attended a performance of *Messiah* himself. Newton displayed only slight acquaintance with Handel's *Messiah*. Frequently he used phrases such as, "If I have not been misinformed," and "I have been informed," or "I have been told." His whole attitude might have been quite different if he had not relied on others for all his information.

Newton concluded his discourses in the spring of 1785, and with the assistance of his poet-friend, William Cowper, proceeded to make arrangements for their publication.

Newton's position is somewhat understandable when we remember that he was among the true disciples of the Puritans who considered music an unChristian amusement, the work of the devil. The most music allowed was metrical psalmody. It was different in Germany. Martin Luther (1483-1546) encouraged sacred music and composed it himself. "A Mighty Fortress Is Our God" still ranks among the greatest hymns. "Next to theology," he said, "I give the highest place to music for thereby all anger is forgotten and melancholy tendencies and many other tribulations and evil thoughts are expelled. It is the best solace for a sad and sorrowful mind."

Newton had advanced to the singing of hymns to simple melodies but he frowned upon all extraneous things, such as elaborate arrangements of music, strong instrumental participation and the like. Even a hundred years later, C. H. Spurgeon, the "heir" of the Puritans, would not allow an organ or piano in his church, but as soon as he died, the congregation had an organ installed.

William Cowper

The distinguished Christian poet who co-authored the *Olney Hymns* with Newton, largely echoed the objections of Newton in a rather sarcastic manner, and somehow could not grasp the fact that a person open to the mind of the Lord could find *Messiah* to be a glorious symphony on the drama of redemption wrought by the "wonderful" Redeemer. The first line of the great hymn by Cowper himself, "God works in a mysterious way His wonders to perform," expresses a truth which the poet would have done well to recognize in his poor evaluation of the *Messiah.*

Cowper, by nature introspective, exemplified a morbid and gloomy tendency, and was rebuked rather sharply by the novelist, Sir Walter Scott: "The charitable purpose of the Abbey performances places the injustice of Cowper's sarcasm upon a level with its absurdity, accusing them, as it does, of a profane and idolatrous tendency."[1]

In *The Village Curate*, the Reverend James Hurdis, in a more generous spirit expressed in his verse what most sincere people felt:

Great soul, O say from what immortal fount
Thou hast deriv'd such never-failing power
To win the soul, and bear it on the wings
Of purest ecstasy, beyond the reach
Of ev'ry human care. From whence thine art
To lift us from the earth, and fix us there
Where pure devotion with unsparing hand
Pours on the altar of the living God
The hallow'd incense of the grateful heart.

---

[1] In our own day, there are not many who object to the great choir and orchestra of the First Baptist Church in Atlanta on television, which so effectively prepares the way for the fine Bible teaching of the pastor, Dr. Charles Stanley. Many who listen, however, would appreciate it more if the clapping were changed to heart-felt Amens.

Whereas Hurdis emphasizes the great genius of the composer, we might do better to see how the music aids in conveying the meaning of the words to the human soul.

General Reaction

The reaction as a whole was mixed. *The Monthly Review* observed that "Newton's discourses contain much real piety, and may be read with profit by all, and, probably with peculiar pleasure by those who are of the party." Most periodicals, as observed by many biographers, "sharply ridiculed Newton and Cowper for the crusade they conducted against Handel's *Messiah*."

Joseph Haydn (1732-1809), a believer, never ceased to marvel "at the grace of God in Christ." For the performance of *Messiah* on June 1, 1791, Haydn had a box near the royal family. "Two of his biographers," William Shield testifies, "write concerning that deep reverence he had for the mighty genius of Handel." To Giuseppe Carpani, Haydn confessed "... that when he heard the music of Handel in London, he was struck as if he had been put back to the beginning of his studies and had known nothing up to that moment. He meditated on every note and drew from those most learned scores the essence of true musical grandeur." (Quoted by Christopher Hogwood in his biography of Handel.)

Von Goethe (1749-1832), acknowledged as Germany's greatest poet, listened to *Messiah* "and was seized by that admiration which repeatedly drew him back to the work during the rest of his long life." Forty years later his enthusiasm was sufficiently well known so that his friends arranged a performance of part of it at his own house. He claimed it as the work which "led me to the most serious in musical art."

About fifty years later, during the Victorian period of the nineteenth century, Newton's discourses continued to create discussion among theologians and musicians.

Charles Simeon (1759-1836) was a learned and godly pastor in the Church of England. His twenty-one volume Bible commentary continues to be published in our day. Though regarded as the leader of the evangelicals, he attended the oratorio *Messiah* and recommended it highly.

Thomas Chalmers (1780-1847), Scottish minister, served with great distinction as pastor in Glasgow and Edinburgh and as philosophy professor at St. Andrews University.[2]

In his seventh and last message of the series called "Astronomical Sermons," he spoke concerning the powerful influence of music like that in the oratorio where emotions may run high, just as they often do at the funeral of a loved one or friend. Such emotions must be tested by experience and practical dedication in doing the will of God and becoming "doers of the Word and not hearers only." Sacred emotions must not be mistaken for solid spiritual progress in daily life and witness.

Dr. Chalmers had nothing but high praise for *Messiah*. "I believe," he said, "that the emotions raised by sublime sacred music here below would have affinity with the emotions which belong to the praises of the upper sanctuary . . . I cannot see why some persons attending oratorios merely for gratification of musical

---

[2]Instead of building only one large church, he kept dividing the large congregation into several smaller ones. In one period of six years, he championed the organization of 216 churches. His sermons continue to be reprinted and there are those in every generation who have been deeply affected by his convincing messages. "The Expulsive Power of a New Affection" is one message that has left a permanent mark on every one who has read it.

taste should prevent all others attending them, who do so from much higher motives."

The most comprehensive response came from Dean Edward B. Ramsay in his splendid *Two Lectures on the Genius of Handel* in January of 1862. He found it difficult to understand the objections, and maintained that "Handel's music is capable of elevating the thoughts," and that "it adds charm and interest to the sublime passages of Scripture. People reading those Scriptures would be that much more able to appreciate and understand them since they were impressed by them in hearing the *Messiah*."

Dr. Joseph Parker (1830-1902), "one of London's greatest pulpit masters" who was pastor of the City Temple for many years, spoke an engaging word concerning music: "It is not necessary that all men should always sing with the voice; when the music is divinest the truly musical soul will be most silent. It acknowledges the kinship of the service; it says within itself, that is complete; that is acceptable to God; my heart swells when I hear it; I thank Heaven for voices so rich and pure and healthful.

"Yet there are times of overflooding, when religious ecstasy becomes supreme, and every old man and little child must have some share in the grand shout.

"Why should the devil have all the instruments of music, and write his name upon them as if he had made them? He never made one of them; he is a thief from the beginning. The devil has nothing that is fascinating that he has not stolen from the Church. There is no genius in evil; there is hardly any talent in it. There is a genius in goodness; blessed are the pure in heart, for that genius shall see God.

"There shall come another day into the history, on which day it shall be said: At what time ye hear the sound of music, rise and pray: it is the Master calling in His sweetest voice; He has left behind the mechanism of mere words, and is appealing to us through the mystery, the magic, the miracle, of tender strains of noble music."

Entertainment and More

Did not Handel write *Messiah* for the sake of entertainment?

Good question!

The librettist Charles Jennens referred to it as an "entertainment." Others referred to it similarly. Handel never called it an "entertainment."

Some days after the first performance of *Messiah*, Handel went to pay his respects to Lord Kinnoull, with whom he was particularly acquainted. "Ah Handel! Handel! This *Messiah* of yours is setting the world on fire. It is a fine entertainment, indeed!"

"Entertainment!" exclaimed the composer, his wig shaking violently, "I do not wish to entertain them, sir, but to make them better."

"If a man can only speak through his harp," Joseph Parker remarked in his discourses on Job, "play it, and we will tell you whether God or the devil stretched the strings, and taught your fingers to discourse upon them. There is a spirit in man, a verifying faculty, a child-heart, that knows what the father said, and knows the very tone in which he said it."

"Entertainment and edification are *not* mutually exclusive, but with much of today's contemporary church music, the entertainment dominates. One could wish that the lyrical quality of the *Messiah* were more the norm of today's music" (Jim Woychuk).

Chapter 11

Handel and His Messiah

There are four chief sources of information about Handel.

The first is John Christopher Smith's *Memories of Handel and His Anecdotes.* In 1717 Handel persuaded his university friend, Johann Christoph Schmidt to give up his wool trade in Germany and to become Handel's principal copyist and head of the scriptorium. John Christopher Smith (his Anglicized name) and his son of the same name became Handel's intimate friends as well as business partners.

The second is John Mainwaring's *Memoirs of the Life of the Late G. F. Handel.* Mainwaring was Fellow of St. John's College, Cambridge, and Rector of Church Streton, Shropshire. In his Memoirs he relied heavily on Smith's writings and it was published anonymously less than a year after Handel's death.

Dr. Charles Burney (1726-1814) wrote *History of Music.* He first knew Handel as a schoolboy, and later joined his orchestra. He formed a life-long admiration for him. "Handel's general look," he recalled, "was somewhat heavy and dour; but when he did smile, it was a sudden flash of intelligence, wit and good humor, beaming in his countenance, which I hardly ever saw in any other."

The last is Sir John Hawkins (1719-89), who wrote *The General History of Music* in five volumes. He came to know Handel in his latter years and tells us that "he was in his person a large made and very portly man." Jacobi, in his biography refines it: "He was stout in the full bloom of his manhood."

But to continue with the words of Hawkins, "His features were finely marked, and the general cast of his countenance placid, bespeaking dignity tempered with benevolence, and every quality of the heart that has a tendency to begat confidence and insure esteem."

Hawkins felt that only Francois Roubiliac, the French sculptor, "caught something of the mixture of ease and alertness which are so essentially that of the great composer." These are evident in the Windsor bust of Handel and the Westminster Abbey monument.

Others speak of him as a man who was vigorous, proud, independent and totally devoid of ill-nature or malevolence. His temper was straightforward and cheerful, but when irritated, he could be fierce.

The elder Smith and Handel were walking along a street in Tunbridge Wells when an argument sprang up between them. Handel's temper was fiery and he never minced words. Smith, well aware that Handel by that time (1753) was blind and could not get along without him, turned sharply on his heels and returned to London, leaving Handel standing in the street. This could be regarded as the result of their ages and infirmities, but nothing can excuse Smith for his wanton act of cruelty. Handel promptly struck Smith's name out of his will. But Handel could not continue with malice in his heart and at length restored Smith's name in the will.

Handel's costume normally included a gold-laced coat with ruffles. He wore the Sir Godfrey Kneller wig—the largest of wigs. It is recorded that when things went well at a performance, Handel's wig had a certain nod or vibration which indicated his pleasure and satisfaction. Without it, keen observers were certain that he was out of humor.

Franz Liszt (1811-86), Hungarian composer and innovative pianist, described Handel, from the information that had accumulated over the years, in a perceptive manner: "Handel seems to our epigonic [imitating] generation like one of the giants of the past. In his life he stands out as one of the most energetic and sublime figures known to the history of art— strong, free, unyielding in his pursuit of an exalted goal; even when he seems to be defeated in the struggle against his own epoch, his mighty spirit rises up to gain fresh victories."

Christopher W. Gluck (1714-87), was a German operatic composer and Michael Kelly recorded significant words from him: "One morning, after I had been singing with him (Gluck), he said, 'Follow me upstairs, Sir, and I will introduce you to one whom all my life, I have made my study and endeavored to imitate.' I followed him into his bedroom, and opposite to the head of the bed saw a full-length picture of Handel in a rich frame. 'There, Sir,' said he, 'is the portrait of the inspired master of art. When I open my eyes in the morning I look upon him with reverential awe and acknowledge him as such, and the highest praise is due to your country for having distinguished and cherished his gigantic genius.'"

Handel never married, but according to Newman

Flower, the early twentieth century biographer, he liked the company of women—those women that loved art. His courtesies, his gentleness to them were extreme. Biographers without exception point out that not a breath of suspicion has ever been cast upon the composer's moral character.

Anecdotes

Returning to England one time, Handel stopped at one of the towns in Flanders and asked permission to play the organ at one of the churches. The organist attending him, not knowing who he was, was struck at once by Handel's playing. And when Handel lead off in a fugue, in astonishment the organist ran up to him, and embracing him, said, "You must be no other but the great Handel."

* * *

Dr. Maurice Greene gave Handel his composition of a solo anthem, which he had just finished. The doctor came back, coffee was served, variety of topics discussed, but not a word concerning the composition. At length Greene said with some anxiety, "Well, Sir, but my anthem—what do you think of it?" "Oh, your antum-ah-why I did tink it vanted *air*, Dr. Greene." "*Air*, Sir?" "Yes, air, and so I did hang ut of de vindow."

* * *

In November 1741, Handel set off for Dublin. Poor weather kept him in Chester for several days. He decided to set up a rehearsal of the *Messiah*. He advertised for local choirmen who could sing at sight. A printer named Jason showed up. Finally, as Charles Burney, who was then a schoolboy and who later loved to report the scene, wrote, "Poor Jason failed so egregiously that Handel let loose his greatbear upon him, and cried out in broken English, 'You shcoundrel, did you not tell me, you could sing on soite?'

" 'Yes, Sir,' " said the printer, " 'and so I can, but not at first sight.' "

* * *

In the summer of 1750, Handel started working on a new oratorio, *Jephtha*. He had to lay the work aside due to his failing eyesight; this happened as he was working on a chorus, "How dark, O Lord, are Thy decrees, All hid from mortal sight." He took the baths at Bath and Cheltenham, but his eyesight was no better. He consulted a surgeon, who was pessimistic, and suggested that Handel go into partnership with the English composer and organist, John Stanley, who had been blind since infancy.

To this suggestion Handel replied: "Have you never read the Scriptures? Do you remember? If the blind lead the blind, they both fall into the ditch." His humor had not deserted him.

* * *

John Taylor tells an odd story: Dr. Morell, one fine summer morning, was roused out of bed at five o'clock by Handel, who came by carriage a short distance from London. The doctor went to the window and spoke to Handel who would not leave the carriage.

Handel was at that time composing an oratorio from a libretto (text) the doctor had prepared. When the doctor asked him what he wanted, he said, "What de devil means de vord 'billow'?"—a word in the libretto. The doctor, after laughing at so ludicrous a reason for disturbing him, told him that "billow" meant wave, a wave of the sea. "Oh, de vave," said Handel, and bade his coachman return, without addressing another word to the doctor.

The Musical Artist in Messiah

Handel's music and the words of Scripture are inseparable; they stand united as one "balanced piece of musical architecture." The composer accepted the words as from God and proceeded rapidly to write *appropriate* music that would effectively convey the full meaning of those words. The Messiah's life and His mediatorial work magnificently unfold in Handel's music—from prophecy to substitutionary sufferings of Christ to the rapture of the redeemed.

Messiah, progressively through the decades and centuries, has been universally regarded as a solid example of artistic excellence. Anna Seward, *"Swan of Lichfield,"* and friend of Dr. Samuel Johnson, describes the composer as "pre-eminent, incomparable, transcendent, unrivalled, unequalled," and made the further observation, "that in music, when it marries immortal verse, and then only is it truly sublime. Handel stands approachless, as Shakespeare himself, in grandeur and variety."

On September 28, 1823, a young Englishman, Edward Schultz, visited Beethoven at Baden. He said, "In the whole course of our table-talk there was nothing so interesting as what he said about Handel. I sat close by him and heard very distinctly what he had to say. I cannot describe to you with what pathos, and I am inclined to say with what sublimity of language, he spoke of Handel's genius in the immortal *Messiah*. Every one of us was moved when he said, 'Ich würde mein Haupt enthlössen und seinem Grabe niederknien.' "[1]

An unexpected appraisal of *Messiah* comes from George Bernard Shaw (1856-1950), the distinguished Irish playwright and critic. Speaking to a society of

---

[1] (I would bow my head and kneel at his grave.)

French musicians, he said, "With *Messiah* I have spent many hours which others give to Shakespeare, or Scott, or Dickens... Handel is not a mere composer in England: he is an institution. What is more, he is a sacred institution . . . That is why every Englishman believes that Handel now occupies an important position in heaven."

Shaw was speaking somewhat after the manner of men, but as to Handel's presence in heaven, this introduces an intriguing subject.

It is quite amazing—although we should hardly expect it to be otherwise—to note how studiously many of Handel's biographers go out of their way to caution the reader negatively about the spiritual scope of the *Messiah* and spiritual interests of its composer.

Robert Manson Myers' otherwise splendid biography exemplifies this pervasive tendency. "Those who seek to glorify *Messiah* with the halo of ecclesiastical fervor," he said, "inevitably rob Handel's positively monumental work of its great musical force. No one wants artifice in place of art. And no sensitive musician wants shoddy sentimentality in the place of critical Handelian enthusiasm."

Jim Woychuk, who has appreciated *Messiah* since singing it in the high school choir, gives an effective response: "While some euphoric listeners seem overly effusive in their praise of the oratorio, Myers' dichotomy is unnecessary. Great art appreciation and profound spiritual edification are not mutually exclusive. Far from robbing Handel's work of its great musical force, a vision of the redeeming Christ at the center of the oratorio's text, magnifies Handel's musical skill. When one considers that Handel had the greatest drama in the history of the universe as his subject, the splendor of his artistic accomplishment is clearly seen. In attempting to paint a fitting musical portrait of the wonderful Savior revealed in Scripture, Handel summons the deepest and best powers of his musical genius.

"The singular reaction from the critics and masses alike testifies to the success of his efforts. Only a theme of such eternal grandeur could evoke music that demonstrated the extent of Handel's abilities. With such a work 'robbery' would be more likely when the critical analyses eclipse the spiritual values rather than vice-versa."

It is refreshing also to read the more rational, and we should say the more appropriate, statement of biographer, R. A. Streatfeild. He describes *Messiah* "as not only a very great work of art, but it is actually the first instance in the history of music of an attempt to view the mighty drama of human redemption from an artistic standpoint."

Handel was brought up in the Lutheran church. He remembered how his forebears fled from the Hapsburg empire "for the love of the pure evangelical truth." No doubt that much of his early training stayed with him through the years. One week after Handel died, James Smyth in a letter to Bernard Granville, said concerning Handel, "He died as he lived—a good Christian, with a true sense of his duty to God and man, and in perfect charity with all the world."

To Handel the three Persons of the Trinity were entities as real as people around him. He attended church faithfully and lived an intense and balanced life. He was not easily swayed by the voices around him.

The Deists ranted loudly in his day. They believed in a Supreme Being, but only in the sense of the original creating force from which material life was derived. They denied the divine revelation of the Bible. They did not believe in supernatural divine intervention in human affairs. The writings of John Locke influenced many in those days.

Handel was stable in his beliefs, and the reasonings of skeptics dissolved quickly in the supernatural light which he found in the Bible.

Chapter 12

The Impact of Messiah on the Composer

When Handel received Jennens' arrangement of those seventy-nine Bible verses on August 22nd, 1741, he read them carefully and studied them intently and long before commencing to write the music.

One writer suggests that while meditating on those Scriptures for so long a time, Handel probably memorized the seventy-nine Bible verses as well as the music even before he completed writing his composition.[1]

The Scriptures always greatly influence the mind of any person who takes time to think upon them carefully. Handel obviously recognized that he was dealing with Words that were infinitely superior to the words of men.

In speaking to his "family" at the Foundling Hospi-

---

[1] Judging from the calls and letters received, there are many today who intend to memorize those Scriptures. With those divine Words in mind and heart, people listening to *Messiah*, whether on tape or live, will be quite literally sitting "in heavenly places."

81

tal, Handel said that as he meditated on those portions of Scripture, he found that "the words seemed to sing by themselves."

The Secret of Messiah's Greatness

Handel seemed to understand the real secret of his oratorio *Messiah*. It resides first in the words he was dealing with—they "seemed to sing by themselves." It is well to recall the statement of the Prince of Wales at the banquet following the first performance of *Messiah* at the Foundling Hospital on May 1, 1750. He spoke of the oratorio as a "divine work of music," and went on to take special notice of the text. "Without that unique compilation from the Bible, the true revelation of *Messiah* could not be achieved."

"The words seemed to sing by themselves!" The "words!" They are God's Words. They are *superior* to the words of men. They are *infinitely* superior to the words of men as the prophet Isaiah expressed it: "For my thoughts are not your thoughts, neither are your ways my ways, saith the Lord. For the heavens are higher than the earth, so are My ways higher than your ways, and My thoughts than your thoughts." Christ affirmed the same conviction, "The words that I speak unto you," He said, "they are spirit and they are life."

Handel heard those words singing by themselves. He caught the melodies and harmonies, as it were, resident in those inspired Words, and set them down on paper.

This is the real secret of the greatness of *Messiah!*

Handel's grand oratorio *Messiah* remains unexcelled to this day, and many scholars venture to say that it will remain unexcelled "until the King of glory shall come in." A generation later, Beethoven said, "To him I bend the knee, for Handel is the greatest, ablest composer that ever lived."

"The greatest composer thàt ever lived" wrote music for the greatest words that ever were spoken concerning the ever-living, ever-glorious Redeemer.

But what else did the musician perceive?

The Finished Symphony

As he studied those divine words from first to last, Handel obviously discovered that they presented—comprehensively—God's great drama of redemption through the Lord Jesus Christ, beginning with its prophecies in the Old Testament and its fulfillment in the life and work of Christ and its future consummation in the return of Christ.

Schubert, the gifted Austrian composer, was working on a symphony, but death prevented him from completing it. What he did complete has great merit, and to this day is known as *The Unfinished Symphony*.

But here in Handel's hands were the words of another symphony. Its theme originated with God in eternity past when the supreme Composer planned the sweet music of His love toward a lost world. Here He would display the riches of His grace and the marvels of His infinite power. The central personality in God's symphony is His blessed Son, the Lord Jesus Christ—the great Messiah.

Prophets foretold His birth, His sufferings, His death and His resurrection. Handel could hardly have failed to see all this. In the fulness of time, Messiah came and fulfilled all that the prophets had spoken. He "died the just for the unjust." He died "for our sins according to the Scriptures." He "rose again the third day according to the Scriptures."

Unlike Schubert who could not furnish the *Finale*, God has in total readiness a glorious consummation to His Symphony of Redemption. Christ promised that He would return to take all the redeemed to heaven. The apostles announced the Finale in glowing terms.

Handel must have looked at those words in amazement: "Behold, I show you a mystery; we shall not all sleep, but we shall all be changed, in a moment, in the twinkling of an eye, at the last trump: for the trumpet shall sound, and the dead shall be raised incorruptible, and we shall be changed."

Handel's Faith

The "words" speak of rapture divine. They were "singing," clearly the finale of God's drama of redemption. Handel heard that music. He said so. He heard the music of God's symphony. His soul was tuned with God, and the wondrously well-suited music "poured out" in accents and harmonies beyond his own capabilities. "I thought I saw all heaven before me," Handel testified later, "and the great God Himself."

In speaking of the time when he composed *Messiah*, Handel said, "Whether I was in the body or out of the body, I know not."

These are very unusual words. Paul spoke these words concerning the time when he was "caught up into the third heaven" and there "heard unspeakable words which it is not lawful [allowed] for a man to utter."

In these rare statements attributed to Handel, one can hardly fail to understand that he claims to have experienced some special illumination in the understanding of these Scriptures.

These strong words of Handel appear in many biographies of the composer. Some prefer to call them mere legends and that they carry no meaning. But a different interpretation is more likely.

Handel never spoke in this manner concerning any other of his many compositions. The origin of these singular remarks goes back to the beginning and must have been circulated by those who knew him, including the elder Smith who wrote the first memoirs of the composer. It appears rather incredible that Smith or any other acquaintance of Handel would just invent such remarks and observations and attribute them to the composer. Rather than disregarding these personal remarks, it makes more sense to accept them and seek to comprehend their meaning in the context where they appear.

At regular intervals Handel's man-servant brought him food, and when he returned he would find the platter untouched. Sometimes the servant stood in silent astonishment watching the master's tears dropping on his page and spreading over the ink, blotching the notes he had penned. This man was obviously very moved concerning the subject of his composition.

While Handel was composing the section which begins with the words, "He was despised and rejected of men," a visitor is reported to have found the composer trembling and sobbing with intense emotion. What was going on?

This is the heart of the Scripture in Isaiah which tells about the extreme sufferings of our Lord when the iniquities of us all were laid upon Him.

Could this have been the precise time when the gifted composer recognized that the Lord "was wounded," but that He "was wounded" for Handel's transgressions; that "He was bruised," but that "He was bruised" for Handel's iniquities?

This is not an effort to "convert Handel into a saint." That is not within man's power. It is understood that this man had faults and weaknesses like any other —more or less—but it is also understood that Handel, like any other believer, could accept the gift of eternal life from God by simple faith, and pass from death unto life.

The poet, Samuel Taylor Coleridge (1772-1834), said, "Faith is an affirmation and an act." This is good!

From early childhood Handel believed in God; he *affirmed* the truth about God revealed in the Bible. Now he was confronted with the Bible truth that the God-sent Redeemer died for *his* sins. If he truly accepted this truth, he went beyond the simple affirmation he had always held, and his faith became an *act*. In this act, he embraced the Lord Jesus Christ as *his* Savior and as *his* Lord.

This could then well be the reason why the composer with "tears streaming from his eyes," could write the "Hallelujah Chorus" so triumphantly and so exuberantly as to make the music reach the ends of the earth.

And when he was seen "staring into space," perhaps he was envisioning the "incorruptible inheritance" which he would soon possess.

The word "perhaps" is used because in the end, only God "knoweth them that are His."

On April 6, 1759, Handel directed the *Messiah* at Covent Garden. As he was preparing to leave the theatre, he fainted. It was Passion Week. When he regained consciousness, he said, "I want to die on Good Friday in the hope of rejoining the good God, my sweet Lord and Savior, on the day of His resurrection."

Only a person who expected to go to heaven would speak such words of confident expectation! Quite naturally a question arises concerning Handel's life as a Christian. If he truly was born again, why did he not witness more clearly to those around him? Maybe for the same reason that we fail in this area. We often hesitate to speak clearly about the Lord to our contemporaries.

Mr. Handel lived an intense inner life, but he maintained a natural reserve about his sorrows, his inward struggles and his triumphs. It is not difficult to understand how he would hesitate to speak about the Lord as he probably had reason to suspect that the reaction of his associates might be ridicule.

How wonderful it would be to read some clear and strong testimony from him about the dear Lord who provided for him and for us all such wonderful salvation!

But is not his immortal music, with each of the seventy-nine Scriptures, a testimony? Handel found those words already singing. He gave them utterance with unsurpassed melody, harmony and the right emphasis. He exhibited his faith beneficially through his works. For some two hundred fifty years his testimony has been ringing out around the world!

Glory to God!
Glory to Christ the Lord;
Glory in earth and heaven,
Glory with one accord;
To Him who earth upholds
By His almighty word;
To Him by whom all things
Have been at last restored!
His is the Name of names,
In Heaven and earth adored.

−Unknown

The Composer's Quiet Witness

Handel was an assiduous church goer and studied the Scriptures with enthusiasm and joy. Sir John Hawkins tells of seeing him at church "on his knees, expressing by his looks and gesticulations the utmost fervor of devotion." Lady Huntington, a vibrant Christian leader among the Methodists, visited Handel a few weeks before his death, and made a significant

GEORGE FREDERICK HANDEL Efq.
born February XXIII. MDCLXXXIV.
died April XIV. MDCCLIX.

L.F.Roubiliac inv.' et sc.

The monument of Handel by Louis-Francois Roubiliac
at Westminster Abbey. Sir John Hawkins thought it had best
mixture "of ease and alertness which are so essentially that of the
great composer." Date on his birth, as it appears, is erroneously
one year early.

entry in her diary: "He is now old, and at the close of his long career; yet he is not dismayed at the prospect before him. Blessed be God for the comforts and consolations which the Gospel affords in every situation, and in every time of our need!"

Hawkins, Burney and others who knew him regarded him as a true Christian, despite some of the things that have been said to the contrary.

It is significant that the oratorio *Messiah* was not designed as one of his economic ventures. The profits from the performance in Dublin, all the performances at the Foundling Hospital and probably others were for the sake of charity. In all likelihood, Handel received very little remuneration from that work throughout his life. *Messiah* was a gift to others! The Foundling Hospital was close to Mr. Handel's heart, and prospered for many years, in part because of his deep interest. The last of the original buildings was demolished in 1926, but the Foundation which Captain Coram established still exists.

Soon after Handel's death the *Gentleman's Magazine*, wrote in part, "He was liberal even when he was poor, and remembered his former friends when he was rich."

Handel fed the orphans, helped the prisoners, ministered to kings and queens, and people in need. He continues to lift the hearts and minds of multitudes in every successive generation and points them to the Lamb of God, "that was slain, and hath redeemed us to God by His blood."

During the night of April 13-14, 1759, Handel died. It was Good Friday, according to his expressed wish.

He was buried in state at the Poet's Corner in Westminster Abbey on April 20th. Choirs of the Chapel Royal, St. Paul's Cathedral, and the Westminster Abbey sang at the service. More than three thousand of the citizens of London and others attended the funeral in mourning the departure of a brilliant composer and a compassionate man.

Over his grave at Westminster Abbey the statue of Handel is seen at full length. Mrs. Ann Eliza Bray, in her biography published almost one hundred fifty years ago, describes the monument further: "The head is marked by strong character and expression. The sculptor with equal truth and propriety placed in the hand of the composer a score of music with the notes and words of 'I know that my Redeemer liveth,' that most touching song perhaps of all in the *Messiah*. I should not envy a mortal who could look upon it unmoved."

Pending the arrival of the Roubiliac monument, which was unveiled three years later, a choice tribute appeared anonymously in the *Universal Chronicle* of April 21, 1759, just a few days after Handel's departure:

Beneath this place
Are reposited the remains of
GEORGE FRIDERIC HANDEL.
The most excellent musician
Any age ever produced:
Whose compositions were a
Sentimental language
Rather than mere sounds;
And surpassed the power of words
In expressing the various passions
Of the human heart.

Chapter 13

Handel's Masterpiece Lives On

The inspired Words in *Messiah* have not ceased to sing.

God's eternal truth, clothed with melody—articulated by voices and augmented by instruments—in the excelling musical arrangements of *Messiah*, has been singing to millions of listening ears and open hearts of humanity around the world for some two hundred fifty years.

There will be many in heaven who will tell how they first were aroused to the meaning of those Words when they heard them in *Messiah*. They were drawn to the truth of redemption by the awakening music, and, forthwith, one by one, they *acted* in accepting the Redeemer as Savior personally.

Handel's *Messiah* is the high point of Christmastide in London each year. It is performed by the London Philharmonic Orchestra and Choir before a tightly packed audience in the vast Royal Albert Hall. It is also an annual production at

Carnegie Hall in New York and in other metropo-
lises throughout the world.

In addition, Handel's "masterpiece" is annually performed—though perhaps with less distinguished performers—in churches, in schools, in
concert halls, over the air waves, throughout the
English-speaking world and beyond.

In this concluding chapter we have some
reports of blessing over the past two and a half
centuries.

In Philadelphia

On July 14, 1790, the *Messiah* was performed
at the University of Pennsylvania. The *Federal
Gazette* and *The Pennsylvania Packet* had identical
reviews:

> In vain might we attempt to express the pleasing
> emotions which we experienced on this delightful
> occasion. Never were the charms of vocal and in-
> strumental music more happily united. The soul,
> attuned to harmony, forgot for a moment its earthly
> fetters, and soared upon the wings of melody to its
> kindred skies. The heaven struck imagination was
> transported far beyond the limits of mortality, by
> the *Grand Overture* with which the oratorio com-
> menced: nor was it suffered to lack throughout the
> entire composition until it rose to regions still more
> exalted in the Hallelujah Chorus.

In Halle, Germany

Messiah was first performed in Handel's birthplace,
the town of Halle, near Leipzig, Germany, in 1803, but
the most noteworthy performance, however, came in
1857, when Jenny Lind, the beloved Swedish "Nightingale" took the leading soprano.

To digress for a good purpose—Jenny Lind (1820-
1887), was an outstanding opera singer. Her range
extended from the B below middle C to high G, and

her modulation and control were in the area of absolute perfection.

But the time came in her Christian life when she abandoned opera, but continued singing in Christian-oriented musicals. Once a friend found her on the seashore with the Bible in her lap. "How is it," the friend asked earnestly, "that you abandoned stage and opera at the height of your success?"

"When every day," was her quiet answer, "it made me think less of this (laying a finger on her Bible) and nothing at all of that (pointing to the sunset), what else could I do?"

The proceeds from the 1857 performance in Halle went not to charity but for a statue—a statue of Handel himself in the marketplace. The residents of the town had the statue of their beloved composer in their midst on the near centennial anniversary of his death. The statue, we are told, is there today.

The Edinburg Review for July 1857, carried a typical mid-Victorian estimate of the spiritual influence and power of Handel's masterpiece:

> It is not exaggeration, so much as history, to point to *Messiah* as almost the only work of art in being, which for one hundred years has steadily gone on rising higher and higher in fame, drawing myriad after myriad to wonder and to tears—untouched by time, unrivalled by progress—to characterize it as a heritage derived from our fathers, which will go down, by its own intrinsic and increasing value, to our children's children—a creation of mortal imagining, which has almost won the reality of an article of belief by its power to adapt itself to all intelligences, to touch the lowliest, to raise the loftiest, to content the most fastidious.

Samuel Butler (1835-1902), the distinguished English satirist, wrote in his *Notebooks*, "Handel has had the largest place in my thoughts. In fact, I should say that he and his music have been the central fact in my life ever since I was old enough to know of the existence of either life or music. All day long—whether I am writing or painting or walking, but always—I have his music in my head."

In Lindsborg, Kansas

In 1880, Dr. Carl Swenson brought his bride, Alma, to Lindsborg, Kansas, a unique Swedish-American community, to help him found Bethany College, a small Lutheran institution for the purpose of training students in that area. Here is a summary of a comprehensive report given by Robert Manson Myers in his fine biography.

Dr. Swenson was a man of vision and purpose. Before the college was even established, he and his wife ordered from New York vocal scores of Handel's oratorio *Messiah*. These were distributed among the townspeople and farmers, and rehearsals were begun.

Few of the people could read music, but gradually they learned their parts. The band consisted of some forty pioneer farm folk. On Easter Sunday of 1882, the first performance of *Messiah* was rendered. People from far and near—with their families—rode in their wagons to Lindsborg to hear for their first time some great music.

It was an immediate success.

Every year until this day the farmers, businessmen, ordinary laborers and college students in the Lindsborg area come diligently for rehearsals of *Messiah* twice each week from January to April.

Some distinguished soloists are now brought in. The orchestra is now composed almost entirely from students of Bethany College. The choir totals some five hundred voices—approximately one-fourth of the total population of the town and area.

Women who do not sing bake barrels of pastries to provide refreshments for the thousands who come from all parts of the nation to be present at "America's Oberammergau" on the plains of central Kansas.

During Eastertide of 1994, *Messiah* was performed in Lindsborg for the 112th time. Some of the performances each year are broadcast nationally.

As the sounds of the glorious "Amen" fade away, the people stream out of the hall quietly, rejoicing in the great Redeemer who loved us and gave Himself for us.

In An Arizona Indian Reservation

Some years ago, *The Prarie Overcomer*, a unique magazine published by the Prairie Bible Institute, Three Hills, Alberta, carried a unique article related to *Messiah:*

"One day a young Indian named Bill Hayes came to George Walker, the missionary on the Pima reservation in Arizona and said: 'Mr. Walker, our choir would like to learn to sing the Hallelujah Chorus.'

" 'But did you ever hear the Hallelujah Chorus? It's big music, Bill.'

" 'No, we never heard it, but we understand it's pretty good.'

" 'Good? Bill it's tremendous! But it's very hard to learn, and it's the sort of thing you wouldn't want to spoil by singing it poorly.'

"Bill just stood there, and finally said: 'Well, we could at least try, couldn't we?'

"The choir members worked hard at odd jobs until they had accumulated thirty-five dollars for the musical scores. The books came, and that same night the choir assembled for their first practice. In fact, the whole village assembled to see the project launched.

"Bill studied the music for a while and then started 'dinging' with one finger on the scarred old piano. What Bill lacked in technique and experience, he made up in infinite patience and determination.

"He picked out the soprano part with his one finger and turned to the soprano section. 'You sing that much.' They sang it over several times. Then the same for the altos, and the tenors, and the basses. Over and over again, then, 'Now, everybody sing that much.' They worked at it for months. The old piano groaned under the one fingered musician. The choir laboured under the 115-degree Arizona heat. They sang a measure at a time, repeated endlessly.

"Mr. Walker said that wherever you went during those months you could hear snatches being sung by youngsters and grownups alike. Children played ball while singing, 'Haa-le-lu-yuh.' The farmer, irrigating his beans, sang, 'For the Lord God omnipotent reigneth!'

"Finally, Bill was at last ready to do a full rehearsal with full accompaniment. They still had never heard the chorus played by an accomplished musician, and had never heard it sung. Bill came to Mr. Walker:

" 'Could you get us a musician to play the piano for us so we could hear all the parts? We want to see if we can do it with all the parts just right.'

"Mr. Walker recruited a music teacher from the state university. They were all waiting when the missionary and his friend arrived. All of the villagers were present on this night of nights.

"The pianist cringed as she tested the old piano; it was tuned one whole note lower than standard pitch. The choir rose in unison putting their music books behind them, stared resolutely at their director.

They gave their best. This was their supreme moment, and they felt all of its exultation—

'King of kings . . . and Lord of lords . . .
And He shall reign for ever and ever . . .'

"They finished, and a sigh of relief swept over the entire assemblage. There wasn't a dry eye in the house.

Both the accompanist and George Walker were too choked up even to speak.

"After driving a quarter of a mile, Walker got his voice.

" 'Tell me, how did they do?' Another quarter of a mile and the accompanist revived—'Oh! Mr. Walker —it was perfect—perfect.' Another pause, and she said—'*How I wish Handel could have heard those Indians sing!*' "

About 1900, in New York City, Elizabeth Cheney produced a somewhat crude but sincere and emotional recitation entitled "Aunt Deborah Hears the *Messiah.*" In this caricature a country girl named Amelia receives an illiterate letter from her "lovin' aunt," Deborah Brownlow Lewis, describing the "glimpse of glory" she recently enjoyed at a Christmas performance of the "orrytoreo" of *Messiah* in Carnegie Hall. During the "Hallelujah Chorus" Aunt Deborah experienced unbelievable rapture:

> By an' by Jesus has come out of the grave, an' all heven is rejoicin' over his victory. They call that part the "Halleluyer Chorus," an' ev'rybody stands up. It made me think of the jedgment day to see the faces, rows upon rows of 'em way up to the seelin'. There was one halleluyer arter anuther. It was airth an' heven ans'erin' back an' forth, saints an' angels gathered together an' we with 'em. We ware goin' up a broad gold starecase, fer they sang over an' over, "King of kings, an' Lord of lords," an' each time on a hire note hire an' hire still, till my poor soul could hardly bear to stay into this old body, an' I held onto the back of the seat ahead me to keep from risin' rite up into the air.
>
> There was more arter that, but my cup was runnin' over an' I didn't take in the rest. Seemed as if I'd risen with my Lord, an' deth an' the grave an' even the trumpet of the angel didn't consarn me. I've made poor work a-tryin' to tell you how it all sounded, but you must hear it fer yourself. I fully expect it will be sung into the next world, an' I shall hev a part into it there, an' sing as high an' as sweet as any of 'em.

Probably a rehearsal of *Messiah* with Handel in front of the young lady

Queen Victoria at Performance of Messiah

J. Wilbur Chapman (1859-1918), Presbyterian evangelist who worked with D. L. Moody for a while in the United States and in England, wrote concerning Queen Victoria's humble reaction to the performance of the oratorio.

"When Queen Victoria (1819-1901) had just ascended her throne she went, as is the custom of Royalty, to hear 'The Messiah' rendered. She had been instructed as to her conduct by those who knew, and was told that she must not rise when the others stood at the singing of the Hallelujah Chorus. When that magnificent chorus was being sung and the singers were exclaiming 'Hallelujah! Hallelujah! Hallelujah! for the Lord God omnipotent reigneth,' she sat with great difficulty.

"It seemed as if she would rise in spite of the custom of kings and queens at that time, but finally when they came to that part of the chorus where with a shout they proclaim Him King of kings, suddenly the young queen rose and stood with bowed head, as if she would take her own crown from off her head and cast it at His feet."

Two Hundred Fiftieth Birthday Celebration

Newman Flower, in his fine biography (1948) tells a different kind of story:

> At the Marktplatz, Halle, Germany, a Handel celebration was held. It was a clear night with cold stars in the sky and a bitter wind. Some thousands of people had gathered about the Handel statue to await the midnight hour which would bring in the two hundred and fiftieth birthday of Handel. Thirty-six uniformed youths held their blazing torches aloft about the statue.
>
> A hundred yards away the church where Handel had learned his first notes on the organ stood out, a creation of white beauty in the floodlights. Musicians waited

in the gallery between the spires to play to the waiting thousands when the midnight hour had struck. A black sea of people seemed to reach across the square to the steps of the church. There was no sound, no movement. But with midnight came a great clangor of bells.

Presently the crowd began to shuffle and whisper. The vast human sea became restless. *Hitler* was expected! He was asleep in the train which drew in to Halle at this very hour, on his journey from Berlin to Munich. Four officials of Halle went to the station to beg him to come —if only for ten minutes—to greet this city of *Handel* in her hour of celebrations. They were told that Hitler slept and must not be disturbed, and the train swept on into the night.

This was in 1935, when the Führer was in the first stages of his madness. The festival continued, and quite appropriately Germany's destructive dictator, who shook the world for several years, was not present, but the German-English master continues to shake it. Burney put it so well, "Handel did bestride our musical world like a Colossus."

Dr. Leslie D. Weatherhead, a prominent Methodist writer, who served as pastor of City Temple in London, reports an inspiring story:

"Martin Luther once said, 'The heart of religion is in its personal pronoun.'

"I once attended, in the Royal Albert Hall, London, a magnificent rendering of Handel's *Messiah* by a choir of several hundreds. The friend who accompanied me was a dear saint of God, then in his seventies.

"When the 'Hallelujah Chorus' rose to its stupendous heights, 'King of kings and Lord of lords,' my friend could hardly contain himself. Tears were streaming from his clear blue eyes, and he whispered to me, 'That is *my* Savior they were singing about.' I shall never forget the delightful meaning and emphasis he put into that word 'my.' "

This is an inspiring testimony—personal, precious, perennial!

Many, many others have responded similarly in all the years since this monumental musical masterpiece was created!

To trace out and record the blessings and influence of *Messiah* in the many million lives it has touched during the centuries would require a multi-volume encyclopedia.

It is well just to realize that honor, glory and praise of our wonderful Redeemer are accumulating for all eternity!

> All hail the pow'r of Jesus' name!
> Let angels prostrate fall:
> Bring forth the royal diadem,
> And crown Him Lord of all.
>
> O that with yonder sacred throng,
> We at His feet may fall!
> We'll join the everlasting song,
> And crown Him Lord of all!
>
> —E. Perronet

Statue of Handel in the market place at Halle, place of his birth. Score of "I know that my Redeemer liveth" in background

Commentary on Scriptures used in Handel's oratorio
MESSIAH

Introduction to the Commentary
on the Scriptures

We have been looking at the man—the composer. Now we will meditate on the Scriptures and behold the living, incomparable Messiah!

The seventy-nine Bible verses used in Handel's oratorio are divided carefully into fifteen sections. This at once makes it easier to understand the scope of these Scriptures and facilitates the study, the memorization and the meditation upon these significant portions of God's Word.

The commentary is exegetical. An effort has been made to keep the expository notes concise and to the point, except in those passages where a background review is essential for understanding the Scripture.

The Scriptures from the Psalms in the oratorio are taken from an earlier translation. We have used the King James Version of all the Scriptures in this exposition. There is little difference in the two translations, and the thoughts expressed are virtually the same.

Some notations on the music are included. The more technical ones have been gleaned in the professional field; the more practical ones have come through the channel of the non-professional, apprehending listeners.

This study of Handel as it relates to the composition of the *Messiah* is written from the viewpoint of a believer in Christ, and hopefully it will bring blessing to the reader and honor to our Redeemer.

Brief definitions of several musical terms are included. This information is gathered from encyclopedias and dictionaries on music.

The oratorio begins with an instrumental overture, which has the same function as a preface would to a book.

Section 1

Messiah's Coming Heralded

The Hebrew word "Messiah" means "Anointed," the equivalent of the Greek *Christos* for "Christ."

Possibly no Bible chapter has exerted a greater influence on the world's leaders than Isaiah forty. Luther poured over it in the castle at Salzburg; John Brown read it in prison at Harper's Ferry; Cromwell went to it for help in the time of storm; Daniel Webster read it again and again when he was crushed and broken in spirit. Great Britain's poet-laureate, Alfred Lord Tennyson called it one of the five great classics in the Old Testament.

For many years the prophet Isaiah warned Judah about the coming judgment. Straight as an arrow, the marker in Isaiah 39:6 points to Babylon: "All shall be carried to Babylon, nothing shall be left saith the Lord." In 589 B.C., the Babylonians captured Jerusalem, destroyed the beautiful temple Solomon had built, and took the best of the population to Babylon as captives.

In chapter 40, a new theme is introduced, and the Deliverer of Israel is announced with a joyful strain filled with hope. The prophet speaks as though he were amongst the depressed exiles in Babylon and beholds the return of the glory of the God of Israel. He calls upon the exiles to awake out of their spiritual stupor and to prepare for the advent of Jehovah.

"Comfort ye!" It is noteworthy that Handel's oratorio *Messiah* begins with this particular portion in the book of Isaiah with the significant word "comfort," which means to console, to infuse new vigor and support. With majestic, ponderous dark tones, the orchestral overture depicts Israel's sad plight for generations. It crescendoes to a plane of hope in the words and music that follow in the recitative.[1]

Isaiah 40:1-2

**Comfort ye, comfort ye My people,
saith your God.**

**Speak ye comfortably to Jerusalem,
and cry unto her,
that her warfare is accomplished,
that her iniquity is pardoned:
for she hath received of the Lord's hand
double for all her sins.**

As he proclaims the message of comfort, the prophet describes the greatness and glory of the Comforter who would—on the God-appointed day—bring about Israel's permanent restoration.

This is so effectively stated in the opening verses of Isaiah 61: "The Spirit of the Lord God is upon Me; because the Lord hath anointed Me to preach good tidings unto the meek; He hath sent Me to bind up the

---

[1]Recitative: The name given to "the declamatory portions of an oratorio." "Declamatory" suggests an impassioned speech. In the recitative the interest lies in the vocal part; the accompaniment reduced to a minimum, emphasizes the rhythms and accents of spoken language (David Ewen, *Twentieth Century Music*).

broken-hearted, to proclaim liberty to the captives, and the opening of the prison to them that are bound; to proclaim the acceptable year of the Lord . . ." It is beautiful to read how our Redeemer read this Scripture concerning Himself in the synagogue (Luke 4:18-19), but He did not read the balance of verse 19 which refers to the "day of vengeance." This will be taken up when Messiah returns (2 Thess. 1:7-10).

"Comfort ye, comfort ye my people"—All humanity cries out for comfort, consolation and that inward strength. All desire peace, but there is no peace for the wicked. Sin has to be dealt with. The prophet's mind is set on Him—the great Redeemer. He will "suffer the just for the unjust." He will pay redemption's price. He will put an end to the soul's restlessness; He will dispel the darkness and drive away fear; He will infuse hope and comfort.

"Speak ye comfortably to Jerusalem"—"Jerusalem" signifies God's people "Israel." Speak comfortingly, lovingly to the heart of My people. Two hundred years earlier, God spoke the disowning words through the prophet Hosea, "Call his name Lo-ammi: for ye are not My people, and I will not be your God." Though undergoing severe chastisement as captives in a foreign land, they are still "ammi"—My people (Hosea 2:1). There is a balm for all her wounds, a cordial for all her griefs; Messiah is at hand. The "God of all comfort" charges His prophets, His messengers to proclaim consolation to "My people."

> "Ask God to give thee skill
> In comfort's art;
> That thou mayest consecrated be
> And set apart
> Into a life of sympathy.
> For heavy is the weight of ill
> In every heart;

And comforters are needed much
Of Christlike touch."

—A. B. Hamilton

"Her warfare is accomplished"—The "warfare" describes a state of hardship like that of military service. Israel's affliction—referring here particularly to her bondage in a foreign land—has come to an end.

"Her iniquity is pardoned"—Her sins are all expiated—atoned for—and the justice of God is satisfied.

In speaking in this manner, Isaiah is "wrapped into future times" and things future are described as already present. That which the mouth of God has spoken is considered as already done. Israel's afflictions are over. Her sins are pardoned. The prophet will describe in chapter 53 the suffering of the Sin-Bearer. God looks at Christ's suffering on her behalf and says, "comfort ye, comfort ye my people."

"She has received double for all her sins"—Jerusalem has suffered enough for her sins, though not more than the sins deserved. The expression here is elliptical, and the true meaning, as the context would suggest, seems to be that Jerusalem's blessings are double—much greater—than all her afflictions which sin brought upon her. This is in accord with the thought expressed in chapter 61, verse 7, or as the apostle stated, "Where sin abounded, grace hath much more abounded" (Rom. 5:20).

Jerusalem has endured what God's displeasure was obliged to inflict, but His compassion is superabundant. He wounds and He heals in His own appointed time. Here is a turning-point from wrath to love—the infinite love of God demonstrated by Christ Jesus. Therefore, His people receive "beauty for ashes, the oil of joy for mourning, and the garment of praise for the spirit of heaviness" (Isa. 61:3).

Isaiah 40:3-5

The voice of him that crieth in the wilderness,
Prepare ye the way of the Lord,
make straight in the desert a highway for our God.

Every valley shall be exalted,
and every mountain and hill shall be made low:
and the crooked shall be made straight,
and the rough places plain:

And the glory of the Lord shall be revealed,
and all flesh shall see it together:
for the mouth of the Lord hath spoken it.

"The voice of him that crieth in the wilderness"—This is an interjectional clause. Hark, a crier! The prophet hears a voice proclaiming the approach of the Messiah. This brings before us John the Baptist, who was "sent from God" to bear witness of the true light, and prepare a way for the Messiah.

"Prepare ye the way of the Lord"—The voice cries, "Clear the way for Jehovah." Then if John the Baptist is the "voice," Jesus must be "Jehovah." John the Baptist preached repentance, but Israel as a whole was blind and deaf, and the Messiah was rejected. Both master and servant were cut off by wicked hands.

"Highway... every valley... every mountain... crooked made straight... rough places plain"—The crier is advancing into the desert and summoning the people —to make the road ready for the advancing monarch. In a show of pomp and power eastern monarchs sometimes had hills levelled and valleys filled to make a satisfactory road for their caravans.

But Isaiah speaks poetically and the metaphors used do not refer to topography as such. The mountains, the hills and the valleys represent the major difficulties—spiritual, political, physical—which fill their minds with apprehensions. Formidable obstacles loom on Israel's horizon, but to their amazement, the imponderable barriers will be swiftly overcome by their wonder-working, covenant-keeping God— Mountains will be levelled, valleys will be filled, the steep and rough places will become a plain before them.

Some commentators in an effort to give meaning to details in this Scripture take notice of Alexander the Great and how his conquests diffused the Greek language among many nations. They point to the translation of the Hebrew Scriptures into Greek (the Septuagint). Furthermore, the unifying effect of the Roman Empire with the construction of many roads leading to Rome is also seen as a preparation for a more effectual proclamation of the Gospel.

"And the glory of the Lord shall be revealed"—The "glory of the Lord" is a theme found throughout the Old Testament and carries over into the New. The Hebrew term comes from a root word meaning "the weight of the Lord." It is the "unfolded fulness of the divine power," especially as it comes through to man in the scheme of redemption.

Though the leaders in Israel saw no excellence in Christ that they should desire Him (Isa. 53:2), His disciples "beheld His glory" (Jn. 1:14).

In this first chorus in the oratorio, Handel shifts to the rhythmic and joyful exclamation of prophecy.

"And all flesh shall see it together"—This passage reaches to the day when Christ returns to earth "as King of Kings and Lord of Lords" (Rev. 19:16). The whole earth shall then be filled with His glory.

"For the mouth of the Lord has spoken it"—The things envisioned—often beyond our understanding—shall indeed come to pass because "the Word of our God shall stand forever" (Isa. 40:8).

* * *

110

*Messiah* begins with an overture in the minor key. The music is heavy and austere as if depicting the centuries of Israel's sad disobedience. The sound of the horns in the background would seem to indicate that Messiah's full victory will involve a pitched battle.

Over the scene of hopelessness and despair, the opening words which call for comforters have almost a magical effect. The gradually swelling solo—"comfort ye"—is a cappella at times, and suggests the picture of the lone prophet heralding the impending deliverance—summed up in the words "her iniquity is pardoned."

The different keys of music possess a distinctive and separate sphere. In this song the listeners find themselves in the clear, sunny upper air of E major— the heavenly prophecy whose first tones of hope in the clear, consoling manly voice are heard: "Comfort ye my people." Streatfeild calls E major "the sunniest and warmest of all the keys. It is the same key in which Haydn so delighted. In that key he wrote the *Sunrise* in his oratorio *Creation*."

"The contrast of the E minor of the overture with the E major of the three following numbers expresses an effect of unusual strength. From the grey cloudbank of the overture, 'comfort ye' breaks through like a wonderful ray of light, musically symbolized by the sunny E major ritornello"[1] (Jens Peter Larsen).

The accompanied tenor solo, "Comfort ye, comfort ye My people..." comes from across the dark centuries of God's dealings with His backsliding people, and sounds like a voice reaching us from far

---

[1] Ritornello: "Where a recurrent musical passage alternates with different episodes of contrasting material" (*Encyclopedia Britannica,* 1979).

out in space. Place and time are disregarded. The striking emphasis on the word "My" in "My people" is pleasing and effective. God declares that they are *His* people. Then the tenor vaults high up the scale to accentuate the word "cry" in "... speak ye comfortable to Jerusalem, and cry unto her ..."

The aria[2] then proceeds to describe musically a prosaic road-building operation. The music goes upward as the valleys are exalted and descends when the mountains and hills are made low. "Exalted" receives special attention.

The chorus is introduced for the first time with "And the glory of the Lord shall be revealed." "The chorus is begun by the alto and then immediately enlarges into the parts; the second phrase, 'Shall be revealed' has a more flowing rhythm. It starts with a tenor, is pursued by a bass, then the alto, then the soprano fill all the world in a swift and graceful play of hide and seek. Again a third phrase begun and repeated in the same way on the words 'All flesh shall see' comes into increased confusion" (Rockstro).

The chorus of joy leaps up and down as if it could not contain itself. It makes much of "The glory of the Lord shall be revealed." It is a significant foundation for the rest of *Messiah*, inasmuch as magnifying the Lord and bringing glory to His name is the believer's prime responsibility. The male voices combine on a monotone to declare powerfully that the "mouth of the Lord hath spoken it."

---

[2] Aria: Italian in origin, "aria" refers to a "self-contained composition for solo voice, usually with instrumental accompaniment" (Erich Blom, Editor, in *Grove's Dictionary of Music and Musicians*, 1954). *Da capo aria* was an important type of aria in the seventeenth and eighteenth centuries. It consists of three sections, the third being a repetition of the first.

Section 2

Messiah's Birth Predicted

Haggai 2:6-7

**For thus saith the Lord of hosts;
Yet once, it is a little while,
and I will shake the heavens,
and the earth, and the sea,
and the dry land;**

**And I will shake all nations,
and the desire of all nations shall come:
and I will fill this house with glory,
saith the Lord of hosts.**

"Thus says the Lord of hosts"—Whatever the Lord of hosts says is true and will come to pass whether we understand it or not and whether we believe it or not. "Lord of hosts" is one of the Jehovah titles. It has the meaning that God is the head of all the armies in heaven and earth.

"It is a little while"—For us this suggests a few minutes, a few hours, or a few years because of our earthbound perspective—not so with God. Time enters not into His computation.

112

"I will shake the heavens... earth... sea... dry land"—Suggests unprecedented earthquakes, involving the heavens and the entire mass of the earth including the deep waters.

"Yet once"—The writer of Hebrews takes note of this word and compares it with the shaking of the earth when the law was spoken by God at Mount Sinai (12:26-27).

"And I will shake all nations"—Nations have been shaken all through history. The world stood amazed at how the U.S.S.R. (Union of Soviet Socialist Republics) was so swiftly shaken to pieces a few years ago. But none of history's governmental catastrophes can compare with the shaking that will take place when the King of kings "smites the nations" (Rev. 19:15).

"The desire of all nations shall come"—People through the ages have yearned for some great deliverer. Socrates and his disciples expressed their need of some divine teacher. "Without being dogmatic we should like to point out that the desire of all nations can only refer to the longing of all nations for the Deliverer, whether they realize it or not" (Charles L. Feinberg).

"I will fill the house with glory"—This could be a reference to the temple rebuilt under Zerubbabel and renovated by Herod, but more than likely it is a description of how the glory of the Lord shall fill His temple in the kingdom age as described by Ezekiel (44:4).

Haggai's words here are in answer to the concern and weeping of the people who remembered Solomon's temple (Hag. 2:3-5).

As is so often true in the prophetic Scriptures, an immediate situation is addressed, but the prophetic declaration reaches far beyond it and speaks of God's final solution (in the millennium) of all the problems and emergencies caused by man's rebellion and sin.

114

Malachi 3:1-3

Behold, I will send My messenger,
and he shall prepare the way before Me:
and the Lord, whom ye seek,
shall suddenly come to this temple;
even the messenger of the covenant,
whom ye delight in: behold, he shall come,
saith the Lord of hosts.

But who may abide the day of his coming?
and who shall stand when he appeareth?
for he is like a refiner's fire,
and like fullers' soap:

And he shall sit as a refiner and purifier of silver:
and he shall purify the sons of Levi,
and purge them as gold and silver,
that they may offer unto the Lord
an offering in righteousness.

This comes in answer to the question of the people,
"Where is the God of judgment," or better, where is
the God of justice? (Mal. 2:17).

"My messenger shall prepare the way before me"—This
appears to be a reference to John the Baptist, who called for repentance.

"The Lord, whom ye seek, shall suddenly come"—This
"messenger of the covenant" is the Lord Himself. The
people professed to *delight* in Him and look for Him,
but their priests were corrupt and the people were
defrauding the Lord in tithes and offerings (Mal. 3:
7-9). They were eager for God to judge the heathen,
but were blind to their own sins. "Suddenly: the Lord
of glory always comes as a thief in the night to those
who sleep in their sins" (Schmieder). The manner of
His coming was not as they had expected.

"Who may abide the day of His coming"—The word

"abide" here means *endure*. This is a reference to the day of judgment, not to grace. "Malachi, in common with other O. T. prophets, saw both advents of Messiah blended in one horizon, but did not see the separating interval described in Matthew 13, consequent upon the rejection of the King" (C. I. Scofield).

"He is like a refiner's fire, and like fullers' soap"—Coming in judgment, the Lord is compared to the purifying of a "refiner's fire" and the cleansing of laundry soap.

"And He shall purify the sons of Levi"—Just as a smelter purifies gold and silver, so the Lord will refine the sons of Levi, who, as priests continued to offer sacrifices for the people, though they themselves had departed from God's standards of holiness.

"An offering in righteousness"—When the priests are purified, they may then offer to the Lord sacrifices in righteousness. Believers in Christ are now God's "royal priesthood." God grant that their lives are such as becometh those who come before Him with sacrifices of praise!

Isaiah 7:14

**Therefore the Lord himself shall give you a sign;
Behold, a virgin shall conceive, and bear a son,
and shall call his name Immanuel.**

"Behold,"—The use of this word is usually the forewarning of a great event or something out of the ordinary.

"A virgin shall conceive and bear a son"—The Hebrew has not *"a* virgin," but *"the* virgin," (and it is so rendered in the Septuagint Greek), which points to some particular virgin, preeminent above all others.

It is true that the word *alma*, rendered virgin, may also be rendered maiden, but every maiden is presumed a virgin. However, the use of the word *maiden* is unwise because in reality not every maiden *is* a virgin.

Of the nine occurrences of the word *alma* in the Old Testament, it is found that in five instances the context throws no clear light on the exact meaning of the word. But in Genesis 24:43, Exodus 2:8 and Song of Solomon 6:8, the reference is unquestionably to an unmarried girl. "Thus, wherever the context allows a judgment, *alma* is not a general term meaning 'young woman' but a specific one meaning 'virgin.' It is worth noting that outside the Bible, 'so far as may be ascertained,' *alma* was 'never used of a married woman' " (J. Alec Motyer).

Luther's remarks are worth noting: "If a Jew or a Christian can prove to me that in any passage of Scripture *alma* means 'a married woman,' I will give him a hundred florins, although God alone knows where I may find them."

Micah, a contemporary of Isaiah, corroborates this prediction with other details such as the place of Christ's birth and the fact that He is "from everlasting." "Micah designates the divine origin of the Promised One; Isaiah, the miraculous circumstances of His birth" (Rosenmuller).

The Holy Spirit with one stroke cuts through all the reasonings of men who dislike to see the supernatural birth of our Lord, and states the fact clearly in Matthew 1:22-23: "Now all this was done that it might be fulfilled which was spoken of the Lord by the prophet, saying, Behold, a virgin shall be with child, and bring forth a Son, and they shall call His name Emmanuel; which being interpreted is, God with us."

When God sent forth His Son to be made under the law, to redeem us from the curse of the law and be admitted into His family as sons, He was made of a woman (Gal. 4:4,5). Thus He became our near-kinsman, with whom lay the right of redemption.

"And shall call His name Immanuel, God with us"—The virgin's son must in some wonderful way be God Himself. "Immanuel"—God with us—ensures that requirement. We believe that the human nature of our Lord was so intimately and indissolubly united to the divine, that the properties and actings of each nature are justly ascribed to the one person of Christ, the God-man. "Behold then the character of Messiah in this prophecy! a man! a God! A divine person in human nature! God manifested in the flesh! Immanuel, God with us!" (John Newton).

* * *

"Thus saith the Lord" is a vigorous declaration in a robust bass, with strong melisma[1] effect on the words "shake," "sea," reaching the expressive climax on the word "Desire," which speaks of the Redeemer. With high drama, the bass goes on to relate the sudden coming to His temple "of the Lord whom ye seek." The orchestra again pauses to allow the pathos of the prophet to be heard a cappella.

Following an instrumental interlude, the bass continues in a more pleading tone and is soon joined by the chorus. "Appeareth" and "refiner's fire" receive melismatic treatment.

"And He shall purify" envisions the Redeemer in action. Toward the end the chorus reaches the propor-

---

[1]Melisma: From the Greek word which means "melody." It describes the singing of one syllable to a variation involving several notes.

tions of a fugue.[2] The fugue, begun by the sopranos, portrays a methodical purification process. The minor tones, repeatedly achieved in the fugue, would seem to describe the searing pain and anguish associated with the inexorable purpose of purification. The voices come together to explain with a crescendo the purpose of the purifying process: "that they may offer unto the Lord an offering in righteousness."

"Behold a virgin shall conceive" is sung by an alto in a solemn, deliberate and intense voice. It is accompanied by subdued instruments without any ornamentation. This is one of the most beautiful melodies in *Messiah*. "It has the tender exaltation of one of Bellini's madonnas with a touch of sacred awe" (Streatfeild).

In connection with the three hundredth anniversary of Handel's birth, Terry Young wrote a general article on *Messiah* which was carried in the March 20, 1985 issue of the *Presbyterian Journal*. On the *Messiah* as a whole, three or four sentences from the article seem appropriate: "Handel succeeds in appealing to the senses through his musical settings and to the mind through the expertly chosen [Scriptures were chosen by Jennens] Scripture passages. In so doing, he goes straight to the heart of Christian thought and experience. Here is more than sacred opera, more than pretty ancient vignettes set to lovely music. For the Christian especially, *Messiah* is a spiritual event of major proportions."

---

[2] Fugue: From the Latin word "fuga" meaning flight, is "a musical composition in which a melody is taken up by successive voices in imitation, so that the original melody seems to be pursued by its counterparts. The first voice enters in the tonic, the second in the dominant; this key sequence repeated for as many voices as the fugue has" (*Lexicon Webster's Dictionary*).

Section 3

Messiah's Glory Foretold

Isaiah 40:9

O Zion, that bringest good tidings,
get thee up into the high mountain;
O Jerusalem, that bringest good tidings,
lift up thy voice with strength;
lift it up, be not afraid;
say unto the cities of Judah,
Behold your God!

"O Zion, that bringest good tidings"—Zion is here personified as one of those women that announce victory.
"That bringest good tidings" is one Hebrew word
which Delitzsch renders "evangelistess." The translation then reads, "Upon a high mountain get thee up, O
evangelistess Zion, lift up thy voice with strength,
O evangelistess Jerusalem." These "good tidings" that
evangelistess Zion and evangelistess Jerusalem are to
proclaim, are wonderfully good. Seek out a hill or
mountain as a vantage ground from whence to do so.

"Lift up your voice with strength, lift it up, be not afraid"
—You have earth-shaking news to tell your "cities of
Judah." Proclaim it courageously and without any
reservation.

119

"Behold your God"—Behold your God! Behold your King! Behold Messiah has come back in triumph and He is in your midst.

The time envisioned here must be the day when Christ appears in Jerusalem the second time to establish His kingdom on earth.

> O Zion haste, your mission high fulfilling;
> Go tell your daughters in Judah
> That Messiah, your Lord and King,
> Now reigns supreme!

This is the beginning of a new day, a day with endless horizons. Human words are incapable.

"A song so vast, a theme so high, calls for the voice that tuned the sky."

Isaiah 60:1-3

Arise, shine; for thy light is come,
and the glory of the Lord is risen upon thee.

For, behold, the darkness shall cover the earth,
and gross darkness the people:
but the Lord shall arise upon thee,
and his glory shall be seen upon thee.

And the Gentiles shall come to thy light,
and kings to the brightness of thy rising.

"Arise, shine, for thy light is come"—This Scripture follows well Isaiah 40:9. This appeal is addressed to Zion-Jerusalem, as to a woman who has for so long been desolate and prostrate, smitten by the judgments of God, and partially afflicted by her own deception of self-security.

Suddenly, she hears a cry, "Arise, shine, for thy light is come." The Sun of suns is risen upon her! The Messiah, the anointed One is in the midst of her. He is risen with healing in His beams. Behold Him! See Him, adore Him, rejoice in Him! The word "arise" is not just an admonition, but a word that connotes creative force which infuses new life into her. Light from above is communicated to His ancient people; it is the light which radiates from God Himself, the light of eternal salvation. Indeed, "the glory of the Lord is risen upon thee."

"Behold, darkness shall cover the earth"—Contrary to some teaching, the time preceding the return of the Lord will be one of spiritual darkness. "For judgment am I come into the world," our Lord said, "that they which see not might see; and that they which see might be made blind" (Jn. 9:39). Those with proud conceit of their own wisdom, hold the instruction of God in contempt, become involved in gross errors, hardness of heart, and abominable wickedness. Those who despise the light of the gospel are taken into "gross darkness" by the evil one. Great apostasy will precede the coming of the Lord (2 Thess. 2).

"But the Lord shall rise upon thee..."—It is Jehovah-Jesus who is rising upon His people, and "His glory shall be seen" upon them. Unfading light and divine glory shall radiate from Zion.

"And the Gentiles shall come to thy light"—The gracious light in Zion—as a magnet—will attract the chastened nations and their kings. They will come to that light for healing, for deliverance and for instruction. This is a vivid demonstration of the words from the apostle Paul in his epistle to the Romans: If the fall of Israel meant the enrichment of the Gentiles, how much more so when His ancient people are restored to fulness, and the glory of God rests upon them! (11:12).

Isaiah 9:2

The people that walked in darkness
have seen a great light:
they that dwell in the land
of the shadow of death,
upon them hath the light shined.

"The people that walked in darkness have seen a great light"—This Scripture is quoted in Matthew 4:13-16. The Messiah, the "great light" appeared, that it "might be fulfilled, which was spoken by Isaiah the prophet." Leaving Nazareth, the Lord went to the land of Zebulun and Naphtali, known as Galilee. The northern part of it bordered on Syria. The people in Galilee associated with foreigners, and were at the greatest distance from Jerusalem. They were lightly esteemed by the other Jews. No prophet, they said, could arise in Galilee (Jn. 7:52).

Upon this people—living in ignorance and "the shadow of death," the "great light" shined. This despised area—Galilee—became the principal scene of our Lord's ministry.

Isaiah 9:6

For unto us a child is born,
unto us a son is given:
and the government shall be upon his shoulder:
and his name shall be called Wonderful,
Counsellor, The mighty God, The everlasting Father,
The Prince of Peace.

"Unto us a child is born, unto us a son is given"—Again the prophet speaks of this future event as though it were present. In describing our Lord's incarnation, the Holy Spirit, speaking through the prophet, takes care to make every aspect clear. "Unto us a child is

born," in our nature, born of a woman, "Unto us a son is given," not merely a man-child, but emphatically a son, the Son of God. This is the God-man, "the mystery of godliness" (1 Tim. 3:16), the central truth of divine revelation. This supreme event of the ages took place almost unnoticed by mankind. When they saw Him, they despised, rejected and crucified Him.

"*The government shall be upon His shoulder*"—This God-man is destined to exercise supreme rule in all the earth so that "the kingdoms of this world" will become "the kingdoms of our Lord" (Rev. 11:15). In the oratorio, this statement is emphasized in the Hallelujah Chorus.

"*His name shall be called*"—These are not literal or formal names given to Him, but names with which the Spirit delights to adorn Him. They characterize Him. They are like the bells on the High-priest's garment, ringing His praise. "His name encircles every grace that God as man could show."

"*Wonderful*"—The word here is *secret*, as it is translated in Judges 13:18. It means "full of wonder," the root meaning of wonderful. Who can by searching find Him out? "No one knoweth the Son but the Father." But those who trust Him and love Him worship the wonder of His Name—in greatness incomprehensible, in wisdom untraceable, in fulness inexhaustible, in power infinite. In all of His words, acts, and life, He is inexpressibly *wonderful*.

"*Counsellor*"—He is the source of all wisdom, the giver of instruction, the revealer of the mind and heart of God. His secret is with them that seek His face in love and adoration.

"*The mighty God*"—Our Lord possesses all the incommunicable perfection of Deity. In Him dwells all the fulness of the Godhead bodily (Col. 2:9). Who else but the mighty God could say, "Before Abraham was, I AM"? (Jn. 8:58).

124

"Everlasting Father"—He is the eternal Father. As believers, we are born into His family by the efficacy of His blood, His Word and the Holy Spirit. He is the everlasting Father and He will never abandon His children.

"Prince of Peace"—As sovereign, "He speaks peace unto His people" (Ps. 85:8). He has made "peace" by the blood of His cross for all them that come unto God by Him (Col. 1:20). In all the storms that engulf us in our earthly sojourn, He alone can bring peace (Mk. 4: 39). Blessed are they who have peace with God and whose hearts and minds are ever guarded in that peace of God which passes all understanding (Phil. 4:7).

* * *

"O Zion, that bringest good tidings": The ascending music dominates, and one can almost feel the strong urging of Jerusalem to arise, to get up and go fearlessly with the proclamation of the good news. The music reflects the light of God's glory risen upon His people who are now singing with joy.

"Behold your God" emphasizes the people's chief need.

"The people that walked in darkness"—The bass solo depicts the painful groping in darkness, reaching for solid footing. The accompanied bass recitative in dynamic voice relates "Behold darkness shall cover the earth." All is in preparation for the mighty chorus "A child is born . . . a son is given" which joyfully erupts and proclaims the immense truth, and almost reaches fugue proportions.

"Have seen a great light"—The strong emphasis on the word "light" is impressive and magnifies the significance of the Lord's coming to earth.

"For unto us a child is born..." "Begins with bright strings on what sounds like a royal fanfare. The musical emphasis seems to fall on the words 'unto us.' The fugue evokes the joy this announcement brings and crescendoes to a mighty pronouncement of the divine titles of the Redeemer. With the singing of each title, the brass instruments join in the melody and tempo, lending the voices extra power and authority. After each title, the royal fanfare of the strings resumes and gives the listener a pause to take in the significance of each title" (Jim Woychuk).

In speaking of Isaiah 9:6, Charles Burney said, "There is poetry of the highest calibre in the music as well as the words of this chorus. The violin accompaniments are of such a peculiar character and the clearness and facility which reign through the whole is so uncommon that each of them deserves to be particularly marked. With every introduction of the words 'Wonderful,' 'Counsellor,' 'The Mighty God,' 'The Everlasting Father,' 'The Prince of Peace,' the string instruments are truly sublime."

In Isaiah 9:6, both the words and the instruments convey the more complete identity of the Messiah as viewed from the divine perspective. Words such as are found in this passage crave inexpressible power to send them out and to make good their profound meaning and their incalculable worth. Handel gives in full what those inspired words demand.

Leigh Hunt (1784-1859), English poet and critic, expresses what we all feel in that music: "Handel utters the word 'Wonderful,' as if all the trumpets spoke together." Mozart once told Rochlitz, "Handel knows better than any of us what will make an effect; when he chooses he strikes like a thunderbolt." After each strike of the "thunder," the string interlude gives each divine title its own fanfare.

Jens Peter Larsen, Professor of Musicology, University of Copenhagen, in a deft sentence, tells how indestructible the basic fabric of this music remains: "There is a grace and freshness about this chorus, a spontaneous, poised strength reminiscent of the harmony of an antique masterpiece: this is music stamped by noble simplicity of expression and perfect mastery of form."

The professional musicians will find the most complete technical analysis of the music in the 1972 edition of *Handel's Messiah* by Professor Jens Peter Larsen.

Section 4

Messiah's Birth Announced

The Lord of glory inconspicuously slipped into this sad world. He was born, not in a palace, not in a temple, not in a fine house, but in a stable where He was laid in a manger.

The birth of Christ is not described, but we are taken to the fields where the shepherds abode by night, and with them listen to the angelic communication concerning the speck of time when the eternal Word became flesh.

The coming of Messiah, who lived in prophecies for centuries, is announced through the shepherds' vision. The announcement of Christ's birth follows the grand prophetic utterance concerning Him in Isaiah 9:6.

The celebration of His birth came from heaven.

Luke 2:8-14

And there were in the same country
shepherds abiding in the field,
keeping watch over their flock by night.

And, lo, the angel of the Lord came upon them,
and the glory of the Lord shone round about them:
and they were sore afraid.

And the angel said unto them, Fear not:
for behold, I bring you good tidings of great joy,
which shall be to all people.

For unto you is born this day
in the city of David a Savior,
which is Christ the Lord.

And this shall be a sign unto you;
Ye shall find the babe wrapped in swaddling clothes,
lying in a manger.

And suddenly there was with the angel
a multitude of the heavenly host
praising God, and saying,

Glory to God in the highest,
and on earth peace, good will toward men.

"Shepherds... keeping watch over their flocks by night"
—Keepers of sheep were on the bottom of the social
ladder—almost held in contempt.

"Abiding in the field"—This is a translation of one
Greek word. It does not mean that the shepherds
happened to be in the field that night. It means, rather,
that they lived in the field. Their home was with their
sheep day and night.

"The angel of the Lord came upon them"—The messenger from heaven came to them with the most amazing
news.

"The glory of the Lord shone round about them"—The
lowly shepherds were enveloped with supernatural
light.

"They were sore afraid"—A new world seemed to
burst upon them and they were exceedingly fright-

ened. The situation here is comparable to that of Elisha's servant when the Lord "opened" his eyes . . . "and he saw" . . . "the mountain was full of horses and chariots of fire round about Elisha" (2 Kings 6:17).

We live very near or perhaps in the midst of an invisible world filled with amazing realities, but they cannot be perceived by our bodily senses. There may very well be multitudes of objects all about us, but we now lack suitable faculties to perceive them. We sometimes wish we could see the protecting angel camping near us. "Are they not all ministering spirits, sent forth to minister for them who shall be heirs of salvation?" (Heb. 1:14).

"Fear not"—The angel of the Lord calmed their fears with a forceful, *no, no, do not be afraid!*

"I bring you good tidings of great joy"[1]—The world was filled with sadness and despair as the Jewish people lived under oppressive tyranny generation after generation. Now suddenly comes the heartening news of great joy intended not for a privileged few but "for all people."

"For unto you is born this day"—This is the kernel— the *fact*—of the good tidings. "The Word was made flesh" (Jn. 1:14). Prophetic declarations since the day in the garden of Eden pointed to this event.

"In the city of David"—This is the *place*—a small village a few miles from Jerusalem. Bethlehem is called "the city of David" because David likewise was born there.

"A Savior, which is Christ the Lord"—This is the

---

[1]Mrs. Florence DeFlon sent an apt illustration: A little boy in a Christmas program had but one sentence to say: "Behold, I bring you good tidings." He asked his mother what "tidings" meant. She told him it meant "news." When his turn came to recite, he was stagestruck and completely forgot his line. Suddenly it came back to him and he exclaimed emphatically, "Hey, I have good news for you!"

Person who is born. He is the *Savior*—not a helper—
the One who confronts all the sin of the world with
authority based upon redeeming power. He is the
Christ—the anointed One, the promised Messiah.
This is the first time the word "Messiah" or "Christ" is
used in the text of the oratorio. He is the *Lord*—the
Sovereign, who is "from everlasting to everlasting"—
the Lord of glory! The three words, "Christ the Lord,"
"define and contain the 'Gospel' as being good news
as to a Person; and as being Christianity as distinct
from religion, which consists of Articles, Creeds,
Doctrines, and Confessions; i.e. all that is outward"
(E. W. Bullinger).

"And this is the sign..."—The shepherds were told
how they could find this person. He is a babe wrapped
in narrow strips of cloth, lying in a manger. All this
seems contrary to human judgment. The Lord of all
the universe, the One whom the "heaven of heavens
cannot contain," is a baby with a manger for His cradle.
Yet, this is the way it was happening. Though infinitely
rich, He became poor for our sakes (2 Cor. 8:9), and
we must ever stand in awe at the immeasurable extent
of our Lord's condescension.

The shepherds found Jesus. They came, they saw,
they believed and they proclaimed what they witnessed. They went on their way glorifying God (Lu. 2:
15-20).

*"Suddenly there was ... a multitude of the heavenly
host"*—Suddenly, heaven breaks bounds. The
divine messengers sweeping down—are praising
God with an appropriate acclamation of this singular
event. Notice the angels in praising God were "saying"
the words, not "singing," as is generally understood.
The multitude of angels may have been there all along;
but, again like Elisha's servant, their eyes were not
opened to see the heavenly host.

"Glory to God in the highest"—Glory to God in the highest heaven, in the highest degree, for the highest exhibition of His infinite plan and purpose in Christ Jesus, His only begotten Son. The angelic host exclaim over the glory of God's goodness, the glory of His wisdom and the glory of His power, but the consummate excellence of His glory can be understood and proclaimed only by those who are the objects of His redeeming love.

"On earth peace, good will toward men"—But how can peace be attained? "There is no peace, saith my God, to the wicked" (Isa. 57:21). Indeed, there is no peace; there is only vicious hostility and war because man is alienated from God.

Godet's rendering of these words is illuminating: "Peace on earth to the men who are the objects of divine good will." This is appropriately the rendering in most of the current revisions. This peace is that which results from the reconciliation of man to God. In them God is well-pleased. When men become the recipients of His favor through Christ Jesus, they become men of His pleasure. This is the only basis for peace on earth.

> Therefore . . . Glory to God in the highest,
> And on earth peace among men
> In whom He is well-pleased!

* * *

The music here exudes the bliss of a pastoral scene. Larsen thinks that this movement derives from the Christmas music of Calabrian shepherds, which Handel may have heard in Italy during his sojourn there. The music changes the atmosphere from the exulting announcements of the prophets to the unlikely

people, places and events of the country town, Bethlehem. The almost sleepy air[1] carried by the strings periodically surfaces some of the pathos that will attend the life of the Lamb of God born in Bethlehem.

The symphony prepares the way for the announcement of the Messiah's incarnation through the vision that came upon the shepherds.

In this announcement, the story is told musically with celestial sweetness in four soprano recitatives, two of them unaccompanied instrumentally. When the music enters, it shimmers with the dazzling light of God's glory. The strings perform as if portraying the soft beating of the angels' wings.

The excitement gradually builds, punctuated by the rich chords of the harpsichord. The sharp sound on "Savior" stresses the melody with appropriate emphasis. "The Savior which is Christ the Lord" is the specific point of this angelic announcement.

"Glory to God in the highest."—As the chorus bursts upon us, first in the distant trumpets and finally with a full-voiced and full-throated ensemble, the effect is overwhelming: "The eternal Word was made flesh": Messiah comes down to planet earth! The orchestral postlude gradually fades into the distance from whence it came. "The emotional-dynamic scheme of this piece is extraordinarily *raffiné*" [ultra-refined] (Lang).

The sustained high note on "highest" paints the majesty of the Most High. The low notes remind us that, while God is "in the highest," earth is a much lower place. Again the brass instruments duplicate the

---

[1] Air (also spelled ayre) is generally a graceful, elegant, polished song where the same music is repeated in each stanza. It is usually an accompanied solo. The music has animated rhythmic subtleness and is used to express deep emotion. Whether in its instrumental or vocal use, the term "air" becomes "distinguished from its Italian counterpart, aria, for practical purposes."

melody on the pronouncement "Glory to God" to lend more power to those words.

The general effects of this chorus wants nothing from the listener except devoted attention in order to be afforded unaccountable delight.

"Glory to God" comes through vehemently as if intended to express to God heartful praise for so amazing condescension of Deity.

Section 5

Messiah's Mission Revealed

Zechariah 9:9-10

Rejoice greatly, O daughter of Zion;
shout, O daughter of Jerusalem:
behold thy King cometh unto thee:
he is just, and having salvation;
lowly, and riding upon an ass,
and upon a colt the foal of an ass.

And I will cut off the chariot from Ephraim,
and the horse from Jerusalem,
and the battle bow shall be cut off:
and he shall speak peace unto the heathen:
and his dominion shall be from sea even to sea,
and from river even to the ends of the earth.

"Rejoice greatly, O daughter of Zion... of Jerusalem"
Zion and Jerusalem, representing the whole nation,
are called upon to rejoice *greatly* at the presence of
their King Messiah.
"Behold thy King cometh unto thee"—Not *a* king, but
thy King, the long-promised, the long-expected One,

thine own King comes as thy Deliverer. It is His legal right to rule.

"He is just, and having salvation"—"Just" has the force of "being animated with righteousness." "Having salvation" is more accurately translated "victorious," or it may be understood as being saved from the grip of death.

The Hebrew here is in the passive voice, and should be translated "victorious," or "saved" (from death). The *Geneva Bible* of 1560, on which the King James leaned heavily, simply reads, "He is just and saved." Unfortunately both the Septuagint and Jerome's Latin Bible, rendered the passive form "saved" as an active, "saving." The King James straddles the issue with an ambiguous "having salvation." In the oratorio, the librettist altered it to "He is the righteous Savior," which appears to be a correct interpretation, but not an accurate translation.

In the Gospels (Matt. 21:5) the line about His victory when riding to Jerusalem on a donkey is omitted because the real victory over death still lies ahead, though at that time it was only a matter of days.

"Lowly . . . riding upon the foal of an ass"—This is how Israel's King presented Himself to the nation. He is lowly, humble, despite the fact that this is often referred to as His triumphal procession. Many acclaimed Him and shouted "Hosanna in the highest" (Matt. 21: 9). The Lord took no notice of the zeal and homage of His friends, because His heart was filled with compassion for His enemies who were thirsting for His blood. "He came unto His own,"—His own world, His own creatures, His own nation—"and His own received Him not," (Jn. 1:11), and in His deep compassion, He laments over Jerusalem (Matt. 23:37-38). Those shouting Hosanna may have shouted "crucify him," a week later!

Thus the prophecy of Zechariah was fulfilled. Our Lord's entry into Jerusalem was in sharp contrast to the pageantry of earthly conquerors or eastern monarchs. See the victor seated in an imperial carriage, attired in splendid apparel, arrayed with costly ornaments, preceded and followed by a long train of attendants, surrounded on every hand by the loud, though meaningless, acclamations of the ignorant multitudes; these are the honors and plaudits for which some men strive. (They cannot possibly conceive of anything more desirable or more satisfying.)

Verse nine covers the first coming of the Messiah. Verse ten takes up His accomplishments in His second coming. The prophet saw them as one event, just as a traveller looking upon the distant mountain peaks which appear to be almost as one, soon finds that they are separated by a far-extending valley. The prophet saw the events as one but between verse nine and verse ten come the centuries of the Church age in which we now live. This age was not foreseen by the prophet.

"The chariot... the horse... the battle bow"—These are the instruments of human warfare, but they shall "be cut off"—discarded—by the Lord when He returns in His glory.

"And He shall speak peace unto the heathen"—Instead of carnal weapons, the Lord "speaks peace" to the nations, just as He spoke "peace be still" to the boisterous waves of the sea. His dominion will be boundless—"from sea even to sea."

Isaiah 35:5-6

**Then the eyes of the blind shall be opened,
and the ears of the deaf shall be unstopped.**

**Then shall the lame man leap as an hart,
and the tongue of the dumb sing:**

for in the wilderness shall waters break out,
and streams in the desert.

Isaiah 35 is a radiant jewel. It is an eloquent, God-inspired poem which delineates the delightful conditions which will prevail on earth when the Lord Jesus Christ is enthroned as Israel's everlasting King and as Sovereign of the whole universe in the Millennium. It will follow the judgment of the nations and the binding of Satan as stated in Revelation 20.

Isaiah 34 envisions the destruction of the nations which is predicted in other prophecies and described in the latter part of Revelation. The indignation of Jehovah is poured out upon all the nations, and the fury of Jehovah comes down hard upon Edom "in the day of their calamity" (Obadiah 10-15). The Edomites are the descendants of Esau, who have been a thorn in Jacob's side throughout the many centuries. In the final reckoning the unerring wisdom of God goes back to the beginning of history.

Now in Isaiah 35—a new day is born—the day of the glory of the Lord has come! "The wilderness and the solitary place shall be glad for them, and the desert shall rejoice and blossom as the rose . . . And the ransomed of the Lord shall return, and come to Zion with songs and everlasting joy upon their heads: they shall obtain joy and gladness, and sorrow and sighing shall flee away" (35:1,10).

Notice at once how this chapter opens with a clear reference to the deliverance of all creation from the curse, as anticipated in Romans 8:18-22. All creation was subjected to futility and frustration in the fall of man. But here we see it rejoicing "with the glory of Lebanon, the excellency of Carmel and Sharon" as it awakens with "the glory of the Lord and the excellency of our God" (35:2).

The verses before us (35:5-6) require no commentary. We simply rejoice with all who have been delivered and are at last satisfied with "the streams in the desert." This chapter gives us a delightful preview "of the earthly side of glory," as William Kelly puts it.

The Bible commentators who do not see Israel as God's everlasting nation are baffled by prophetic utterances as in Isaiah 35. We must not fail to observe that illustrations, as we may term them, of this blessed deliverance were witnessed when our Lord was on earth. Those who came into contact with Him were affected by His redemptive power. Did not the blind see, the deaf hear, and the lame leap? Surely they did. They are among the first fruits of things to come when the glory of the Lord shall be fully revealed on the earth.

Oh glorious Day!

Isaiah 40:11

He shall feed his flock like a shepherd:
he shall gather the lambs with his arm,
and carry them in his bosom,
and shall gently lead those that are with young.

"He shall feed his flock like a shepherd"—Believers are His people and the "sheep of His pasture" (Ps. 100:3), and He, "the Mighty God," styles Himself as "the good shepherd," who will lay down "His life for the sheep" (Jn. 10:11).

A sheep is a weak, defenseless creature, prone to wander astray, and is seldom able to return of its own accord. The sheep has neither strength to fight, nor speed to escape from the wolf. The "good Shepherd" guides them by His example, by His word, by His providences. He provides for them, He guards them from enemies on every hand and protects them from the unseen "powers of darkness." He revives them, heals them, restores them.

"He shall gather the lambs... and carry them"—Those who are unable to keep pace with the flock He takes in His arms and carries them in the bosom of His cloak. What blessed encouragement this is for the children, young people and the young converts who are weak, unsettled and inexperienced!

"And shall gently lead those that are with young"—The "good Shepherd" will disallow the burdened among His flock to be hurried and tempted beyond what they are able to bear. He is mindful of the parents and their anxieties for their children.

Matthew 11:28

**Come unto me,
all ye that labour and are heavy laden,
and I will give you rest.**

"Come unto me all ye that labor and are heavy laden"—"Come"—there must be a movement—away from idols and snares—come to the Savior. "He that cometh to Me," our Lord said, "shall never hunger, and he that believeth in Me shall never thirst" (Jn. 6:35). "Him that cometh to Me I will in no wise cast out" (Jn. 6:37). Some were willing to search the Scriptures and yet not come to Him. They were unwilling to come to Him to have life given to them (Jn. 5:39,40). Coming to Christ means *believing* that He is able to do what He promises. Note the little word *all*—"It is a little word," says Trapp, "but of large extent." Christ's invitation is unlimited because His atonement and His power are unlimited.

Our dear Lord here compares sinners to poor, toiling animals, laboring in the yoke, and which are at the same time carrying almost intolerable loads like beasts of burden. Every sin they commit and every time they slight the Lord only increases their crushing load.

"And I will give you rest"—For the unsaved who come to Christ there is instant relief from sin's penalty and power. A sweet calm immediately invades the soul. For the believer who will but draw near to Christ there is both rest and refreshment—"a heart at leisure from itself."

Matthew 11:29-30

Take my yoke upon you, and learn of me;
for I am meek and lowly in heart:
and ye shall find rest unto your souls.

For my yoke is easy, and my burden is light.

"Take My yoke upon you, and learn of Me"—The Lord binds up the broken hearts and says sweetly to His own, "Take My yoke upon you"—we are not to be idlers. "To take the yoke of Christ is to give oneself up wholly to His discipline" (Bengel). "Learn of Me," He says, and be instructed "how you should work, and what you should work, and what you should work for, and whom you should work for" (James Morison).

"For I am meek and lowly in heart"—The Lord is not overbearing. He does not drive His children for personal gain. He is gentle and always intent upon their good. In such service there is joy and refreshment for the soul. In coming to Him, rest is given; in serving Him, rest is found.

"My yoke is easy, and My burden is light"—The most satisfying rest is a life in harmony with God's will, and the consciousness of doing His bidding. The yoke of Christ is sweet peace. The burden of Christ is "light." His yoke is lined with love, and His "burden" is pervaded with gratitude. Meekness makes the yoke easy, lowliness of heart makes the burden light.

* * *

"Rejoice greatly" is an exuberant aria where the soprano carries the emphasis to some of the highest registers and the strength of it would seem intended to awaken in a convincing manner those in a deep slumber of unconcern. The word "rejoice" receives fervent Handelian melisma.

"He shall feed His flock"—The soprano solo provides the quintessence of loving compassion—the very motherly quality which makes it convey the care and tenderness of Christ the Good Shepherd. The gently lilting modulation of the music imitates the gentle ways of the Good Shepherd.

"Come unto me . . ."—A solo carries these words of the Messiah Himself with exalted music. Then the chorus speaks for His people who are now a liberated flock. They have been delivered from the yoke of sin and guilt, and now rejoice in the easy yoke of God's grace.

In the chorus the Savior is speaking with gentle solicitude and implores the alienated and estranged to come to Him for true rest.

The melisma emphasis in places reaches the ornamentation of a coloratura.[1]

This marks the end of Part I in the oratorio. It began with the promise of comfort. It ends with the fulfillment of that promise and an invitation to receive the One who made the promise.

---

[1] Coloratura: From Latin *coloratus* (to color). Elaborate embellishments in vocal music.

Section 6

Messiah
Bearing Our Sin

John 1:29

**The next day
John seeth Jesus coming unto him,
and saith, Behold the Lamb of God,
which taketh away the sin of the world.**

"Behold the Lamb of God"—In expecting the Messiah, the religious leaders were looking for some mighty king who would deliver them from the Roman yoke, but the Holy Spirit, speaking through John the Baptist, is presenting to Israel the "Lamb of God" who must first deal with the sin problem. Standing before them is the One whom all the Old Testament sacrifices foreshadowed. He is typified in Abel's sacrifice (Gen. 4). He is seen in that critical moment when Abraham was about to sacrifice Isaac (Gen. 22:12-13). He is seen again in the slain paschal lamb when Israel was delivered from Egypt. In Isaiah 53, the Lord is personified and "brought as a lamb to the slaughter" (53:7). "The Lamb of God" is the fulfillment of all types and figures in the Old Testament.

"His only righteousness I show,
  His saving truth proclaim;
'Tis all my business here below
  To cry, 'Behold the Lamb!'

"Happy, if with my latest breath
  I may but gasp His name;
Preach Him to all, and cry in death,
  'Behold, behold the Lamb!' "

"Which taketh away the sin of the world"—The word for "taketh away" in the Greek is *airein*, which sometimes signifies "to lift," sometimes "to take away." In order to take away sin, it was necessary that the Lord should begin by first taking upon Himself the burden of sin—provide an expiatory sacrifice—and thus lift it and take it away. It appears that both meanings of the word are here incorporated.

The Old Testament sin offerings "covered" *(kaphar)* the sin; the expiatory sacrifice of our Lord *takes sin away.* Christ's substitutionary death takes away sin's penalty, and for those who receive Him as Savior, He is daily purging, cleansing and taking away sin (1 John 1:7-9).

Years ago, the distinguished Dr. Harry Rimmer spoke at the First Baptist Church in Shreveport, Louisiana. He gave an apt illustration on this vital subject.

He was a special speaker at the annual Bible Conference at Winona Lake, Indiana. He had been there all week. On Sunday morning he put on his white suit and walked over to the "Eskimo Inn" for breakfast. He sat at the counter and noticed that they had fresh boysenberries. His order was promptly filled. With eager anticipation, he lifted the first spoonful toward his mouth. At that moment a friend walked toward him from behind, slapped him on the shoulder, and said, "Hello Harry, it's so wonderful to see you again."

You are exactly right! The boysenberries landed on the sleeve of his white suit. He went to his hotel room pondering what he could do. He spied his liquid white shoe polish. Ah, this will work, he said to himself. He covered the blotch on his sleeve. After it dried he did it again, and then again and again. He was happy in his clever achievement.

On Monday he took the jacket to the dry cleaners, and they *removed* the stain. He had covered it with white shoe polish as the blood of animal sacrifices in the Old Testament covered sin. But here the slain Lamb of God removes the sin and *takes it away* "as far as the east is from the west" (Ps. 103:12).

Hallelujah, what a Savior!

Isaiah 53:3

He is despised and rejected of men;
a man of sorrows, and acquainted with grief:
and we hid as it were our faces from Him;
He was despised, and we esteemed Him not.

In Isaiah chapter 53, Christ is presented as the sinless, suffering Substitute for sinful men, who voluntarily took upon Himself the sin of the world (2 Cor. 5:21; Rom. 5:8) so that His divine righteousness might be imputed to those who believe in Him.

"He was despised and rejected of men"—Christ was an object of general contempt, particularly to the Scribes and Pharisees, who were the public authorities and teachers. People generally were intimidated and silenced by the ecclesiastical powers.

"A man of sorrows"—"He was a man of pains, who is intimately acquainted with disease, who has, as it were, entered into a covenant of friendship with it" (Hengstenberg). Failing to perceive how personally

the Lord felt the weight of the people's sin and sorrow, they shunned Him like a Gehazi or Uzziah under the ban of leprosy. In His experience of sorrow, His humanity is blessedly clear to us.

"Acquainted with grief"—He was grieved by the wickedness and insensibility of those with whom He conversed, not to say anything about the intimate knowledge He has of man's evil heart, which is hidden from us. Grief was ever His close companion, and He could well repeat the words with an emphasis peculiar to Himself, "I beheld the transgressors, and was grieved" (Ps. 119:158).

"We esteemed Him not"—We esteemed Him as nothing; we covered our faces that we might not see Him.

Handel carefully avoids any reference to the physical side of the human tragedy, insisting rather on its inner meaning. We are invited not to contemplate the bodily suffering of Jesus but the mystery of the atonement. It is not simply a human Christ (though indeed He was human) who is stricken, scourged, scorned and vilified. Before us is the eternal Son of God.

It is the contrast between Christ's mental agony and the scoffing of the crowd of unbelievers that forms the subject of the picture.

Isaiah 50:6

I gave my back to the smiters,
and my cheeks to them that plucked off the hair:
I hid not my face from shame and spitting.

This verse together with those that follow is part of a soliloquy of the Messiah. In it He dwells upon the sufferings which He would endure as the Redeemer. In connection with the humiliation at the hands of man, He expresses His confidence that God would sustain His *servant*. The detail with which Isaiah describes Christ's suffering attests to the supernatural nature of the prophecy.

"*I gave my back to the smiters*"—In His infinite love, the Lord willingly gave His back to the Satan-inspired cruelties of men, yea, and beyond that, He was smitten by the Father as He stood in the sinner's place and died "the just for the unjust."

"*My cheeks to them that plucked off the hair*"—This detail is not recorded in the Gospels although it likely had a literal fulfillment.

"*I hid not my face from shame and spitting*"—He was treated with meanest contempt when the servants of the High Priest and then the Roman soldiers spit upon Him (Matt. 26:67; 27:26). They would not even think of spitting on Alexander the Great or upon Caesar, but they spit on the Lord of glory! He was insulted. He was mocked. He was reviled, but He reviled not. How solemn all this! What a picture of a holy God in the hands of wicked men! When the apostle Paul would instruct believers to endure suffering patiently, he says, "Consider Him"—he uses here a word which is a mathematical term denoting a ratio or proportion. "Consider Him who endured such contradiction of sinners against Himself, lest ye be wearied and faint in your minds" (Heb. 12:3). Compare yourself with Him, and compute your sufferings in the light of His. Consider who He is, no less than what He endured.

In the verses that follow in Isaiah 50, we read how the Lord expressed confidence in the Father for help and deliverance, and it is instructive to find that the apostle Paul, in Romans 8:33-34 utilizes these same words to give the believer full assurance and hope of eternal salvation.

Isaiah 53:4-5

Surely he hath borne our griefs,
and carried our sorrows:
yet we did esteem him stricken
smitten of God, and afflicted.

But he was wounded for our transgressions,
he was bruised for our iniquities:
the chastisement of our peace was upon him;
and with his stripes we are healed.

Though written by the prophet Isaiah over seven hundred years earlier, the words in this unusual chapter sound as if the writer were right there on the scene at Calvary, beholding our Lord's suffering. In one view is seen both the unspeakable evil of man's sin and the unsearchable riches of God's mercy.

"Surely . . ."—This word is the "verily"—truly—adopted in the New Testament, and which was so much on the lips of our Lord. It expresses the strongest affirmation. None must have the slightest question as to the cause of those indescribable sufferings of our Lord.

"Surely He hath borne our grief and carried our sorrows"—More accurate translation: "He has borne our diseases and our pains," as Delitzsch has it. He bore the full weight as well as the full consequences of man's sin.

Pause here to note that *twelve times over* within the space of this short chapter, the prophet asserts in an emphatic reiteration that all the Lord's sufferings—voluntary and vicarious—were borne *for man*, in order to deliver man from sin and its consequences.

When the Lord delivered someone from disease during His earthly sojourn it was because He was about to pay the full price for what sin's consequences entailed. When someone endures the suffering which another would justly be required to bear, this is called *substitution*. Christ died a substitutionary death—something which is utterly unintelligible to the most intelligent of unbelieving men.

Important question here: Does this mean, therefore, that God's children should now be free from sickness or be always delivered from sickness? The answer is *no* because our bodies are still under the power of *death* (Rom. 8:10) and in them sin is still present, else why are believers instructed to mortify the deeds of the body (Rom. 8:13)? Certainly God heals people frequently in answer to prayer, but not always, else believers would be immortal.

Our perfect bodies are paid for but not yet delivered! With the apostle Paul and with all believers—yea and with all creation—we "groan within ourselves" awaiting that blessed moment—namely "the redemption of the body"—when all the redeemed will be "manifested" and presented in their new "outfits" (bodies) (Rom. 8:19-23). We will all look good—see well, hear well, run well, shout and sing well, and never stop praising God. Oh what a day that will be! Our sicknesses and sufferings and pains are not "worthy to be compared with the glory" and blessedness that will envelop us for years and for millenniums and for endless eternity!

"Truly, truly He has borne our diseases and our pains!"

"Yet we did esteem Him stricken, smitten of God and afflicted"—People in their blindness imagined that He was smitten of God for His own sin—which ought to have been hideous, judging by the severity of His sufferings! To one only, and him as yet not one of the believers, was it given to see the contrary and to cry aloud, "Certainly this was a righteous man" (Lu. 23: 47).

"But He was wounded for our transgressions..."—Our Lord was wounded—pierced—for transgressions, but they were *our* transgressions. He was bruised—crushed—by iniquities, but they were *our* iniquities. The psalmist, speaking in the spirit of prophecy, in the person of the Messiah Himself, says, "They pierced my hands and my feet" (Ps. 22:16). The chastisement or punishment which leads to our peace fell upon Him. By His severe pain, by His scars we are healed.

Contemplate the summarization of this verse by the beloved expositor, John Brown of Haddington (1722-1787): "This verse is a wonderfully complete representation of the sufferings of Jehovah's righteous Servant. The great truth may be thus stated: The numerous, varied, violent, severe, fatal suffering of our Lord, were the endurance of those evils in which God expresses His displeasure at sin, in the room of those who had merited them; and were intended, and have been found effectual, for the expiation of guilt and the obtaining of salvation."[1]

The truth rings out loud and clear. Christ "bore our sins in His own body on the tree" (1 Pet. 2:24), and no ingenuity of man can ever torture these words to express any other meaning.

A man deeply concerned about his soul began reading the Bible. He carefully read through all the books beginning with Genesis. When he came to Isaiah the fifty-third chapter, these words arrested his attention, "With His stripes we are healed." "Now I have found it," he said: "Here is the healing I need for my sin-sick soul, and I see how it comes to me through the sufferings of the Lord Jesus Christ. Blessed be His name! I am healed."

---

[1] Jean Sherman sent a greeting card with redemption truth concisely stated: "He came to pay a debt He did not owe because we owed a debt we could not pay."

Isaiah 53:6

All we like sheep have gone astray;
we have turned every one to his own way;
and the Lord hath laid on him
the iniquity of us all.

"All we like sheep have gone astray . . ."—Sheep are
but dumb and helpless brutes who wander astray and
become easy prey for the ferocious predators. Unlike
the sheep, man is a rational creature and yet "like
sheep" he rebels against the wise counsel of the good
Shepherd and wanders astray.

All men are rebellious wanderers. "There is none
righteous, no not one" (Rom. 3:10). All are in a state of
error, misery, danger and helplessness in their aliena-
tion from God. Not only has man wandered from God,
but everyone has gone in his own direction. Selfish-
ness reigns and men do not unite; instead they quarrel
about everything. Continuous hostility and war
prevail.

Man's errors are willful errors. Man's transgressions are willful transgressions. Man's miseries are
self-inflicted. This iniquity, this guilt must be dealt
with in a way that will satisfy the demands of a holy
and righteous God.

"And the Lord hath laid upon Him the iniquity of us all"
—Jehovah actually made the iniquities of mankind to
fall on Christ. It was like a hostile attack upon Him,
and in the prophetic words of the psalmist, He cried,
"For innumerable evils have compassed me about:
mine iniquities have taken hold upon Me, so that I am
not able to look up; they are more than the hairs of
mine head: therefore my heart faileth Me" (40:12). It
would seem impossible that all the world's sin could
be heaped on one man until we remember that this
was the God-man.

"And He is the propitiation for our sins: and not for ours only, but also for the sins of the whole world" (1 Jn. 2:2) — Imagine all the iniquities of mankind laid upon Christ by God. Imagine the size and weight of them all. All this weight was "laid upon Him," the sinless Son of God. We can hardly comprehend this. It is as "If God should cause the iniquities of us all to meet, as myriads of foul, black sewers might meet, and in one awful, rushing, roaring, filthy, malodorous flood empty themselves at one spot—on Him, the dearest object of [God's] heart" (F. C. Jennings, 1847-1948).

H. A. Ironside (1876-1951), a beloved teacher at seminary whose simple Bible exposition endeared him to many, said, "In Isaiah 53:6, we have the entire story of the Bible epitomized: Man's ruin both by nature and practice, and God's marvelous and all-sufficient remedy. The verse begins with *all* and ends with *all*. An anxious soul was directed to this passage and found peace. Afterward he said, 'I bent low down and went in at the first *all*. I stood up straight and came out at the last.' The first is the acknowledgement of our deep need. The second shows how fully that need has been met in the Cross of Christ."

Thomas Chalmers (1780-1847), Scottish minister, did an unprecedented work for the Lord in Glasgow, but he preached for several years before he became a believer himself. Then he saw the truth of this Scripture, received Christ and became a true gospel preacher. He said on one occasion, "Never did light and peace so fill my mind as when with the simplicity of a little child I realized the blessed import of those words, 'The Lord hath laid on Him the iniquity of us all.' "

Beloved, let us read and memorize Isaiah 53 on our knees!

* * *

This section begins the second part of the *Messiah* which details the sufferings and death of Christ in behalf of sinners.

The opening instrumental notes at once introduce the deep pathos that describes this section.

"Behold the Lamb of God" is sung with majestic solemnity and moves slowly, suggesting laboriousness as the heavy weight of sin is laid upon our blessed Lord. The marked rhythms express the deep pathos, but the mood changes when the purpose of the Lamb's death is explained. There is hopeful confidence, beginning in the music of "taketh away the sin of the world."

The violins seem to echo the soloist like drops of falling tears.

"There *is* truth," Beethoven is reported to have said on his death-bed, " 'Behold the Lamb of God' suggests that truth."

Isaiah, chapters 40 through 53, form the highest peaks of Messianic prophecy in the Old Testament. In these chapters the Servant Songs are given, and the term "servant" occurs some nineteen times.

"He was despised . . ."—The music is measured, slow, somber, filled with divine pathos. The alto aria in short gasps—"despised," "rejected," "griefs,"—accentuates the sorrowful, subdued lament in tender mourning. The melody is emphasized by the inserted counter-replies of the orchestra. Mrs. Cibber, for whom this original aria was intended, was able to express the strongest possible emotion without resorting to superficial exaggeration.

"Surely He hath borne our griefs"—Making the word "surely" tri-syllabic helps the chorus to emphasize the thought. Some hear in the music the idea of lifting a weight as they do also in "Taketh away the sin of the world."

"And with His stripes we are healed"—A fugue of an earlier generation. By repeating the short quotation, the words are pounded into the listener as the essential point of the matter. The music lingers on the word "healed" as though some soothing medication were laid on the wounds.

Handel's music erupts with the glorious drama of Christ's passion. In the penetrating sweet music of the chorus, the listener hears the down-flow of sorrow and love of which Isaac Watts wrote in *When I survey the wondrous cross*. "In one of the loveliest tenor lines in all of choral music one hears the mixture of awful sorrow and contrite gratitude—sorrow at the death of One so pure and lovely, gratitude that '*surely* He *hath* borne our griefs, He *hath* carried our sorrows, He *was* wounded for *our* transgressions, and the chastisement of our peace *was* upon Him.' Hallelujah!" (Jim Woychuk).

"All we like sheep"—The rapid melisma sounds like the sad bleating of wayward sheep. The tone shifts abruptly and dramatically with the entry of the grave bass voices singing, "And the Lord hath laid on Him." The slowing of the music at least suggests attempts at depicting the unfathomable weight of the world's sin being laid on one loving and innocent Person.

"Have gone astray"—This chorus also depicts "meandering figurations," which are particularly effective on the word "turned," sung in rolling counterpoint.

"And the Lord hath laid on Him the iniquity of us all"—The Lord's grief is emphasized, and we are made to see our miserable complicity. The sheep-like shilly-shallying and vacillation of man in his utter inability to bear his own responsibility, depicted by the music, is a well-done background for the far-reaching, somber announcement of the chorus trilogy that God "hath laid on Him [Christ] the iniquity of us all." This is the *central theme* of redemption. However, no music or words can adequately convey the magnitude of what took place, for as the contemporary songwriter Michael Card writes, "No chord is foul enough to sing the pain."

Section 7

Messiah
Enduring Our Death

This section could more accurately be stated: Messiah enduring our *eternal* death.

Psalm 22 begins with a sob and ends with a song. It was the cry of our Lord's darkest hour. This uttermost solitude of forsakenness is a depth we can never sound or experience, because the dear Lord endured it *for* us. To each of His own He says, "I will never leave thee nor forsake thee" (Heb. 13:5).

Commentators are quite unanimous in saying that Psalm 22 applies entirely, directly and—for the most part—exclusively to Christ.

William H. Plumer said, "This Psalm may be called The Gospel According to David." It is indeed the gospel according to David which the Spirit of Christ who was in David did "signify" (1 Pet. 1:11).

Puritan commentator, Trapp, asks, "Is this prophecy or history?" It is prophecy minutely fulfilled in history.

Psalm 22 begins with the words, "My God, my God, why hast Thou forsaken Me?" and according to

156

some careful exegetes, it ends with "It is finished!" These two statements along with five others were the words audibly spoken by our Lord while hanging on the cross, and in all likelihood, every word of this Psalm went through the mind of our dear Savior as He agonized there on that cruel tree in our stead.

As we read it slowly, should not every word open fresh springs of gratitude and fountains of love for our wonderful Redeemer?

Alfred Edersheim (1825-89), in words which appear contradictory calls this "A Psalm of believing despair."

Psalm 22:7-8

All they that see me laugh me to scorn: they shoot out the lip, they shake the head saying,

He trusted on the Lord that he would deliver him: let him deliver him, seeing he delighted in him.

"All they that see Me laugh Me to scorn"—"All"— Jews and Gentiles, priests and people, soldiers and civilians—all united in their unrestrained, hateful derision and cruel mockings of our Lord. Nothing seems to increase the intensity of suffering like the laughter of a bystander.

"They shoot out the lip, they shake the head"—These were the old gestures of contempt—base signs of disdain and disgrace. Compare Matthew 27:39, 43; Mark 15:29; Luke 23:35-36.

"He trusted on the Lord... let Him deliver Him now"— This diabolical strike was aimed at our Lord's faith and confidence in God the Father.

"Seeing He delighted in Him"—With biting sarcasm they taunted the Lord. Since your Father delights in

You, surely He will deliver You. This peculiar venom was intended to torment the Lord in His agonizing hours of dying for the sins of the world.

In all this, we must always try to keep in mind the reality—yea, the mystery—of the three persons in the Godhead. So it was that when Christ suffered alone, yet at the very same time "God was in Christ reconciling the world unto Himself" (2 Cor. 5:19).

Psalm 69:20

Reproach hath broken my heart;
and I am full of heaviness:
and I looked for some to take pity,
but there was none;
and for comforters, but I found none.

There is a close resemblance between Psalm 69 and Psalm 22. Both are written by David.

"Reproach hath broken my heart"—A broken heart in Scripture is a figure for violent and distressing anguish of mind. To Christ's pure mind the vile accusations alone were grievous in the highest degree, but there was more in that, as Sin-bearer, He was enduring the rebuke of God the Father.

Stephen and all the martyrs since then have suffered for Christ's sake scourgings and tortures without a groan and often with rejoicing, but in all their extremities they had the support and enabling of God; they "endured, as seeing Him who is invisible" and had the sense of His presence and consolation.

The Lord Jesus Christ died alone. His death was one of universal solitude. The presence and comfort of God the Father was suspended while He died as a man bearing the iniquities of the whole world. He knew what it was to be abandoned by God that believers might never know it. This entailed not only the withdrawal of the Father, but there was superadded the conscious knowledge of the Father's displeasure. All this is beyond man's limited understanding. One reason is that we comprehend so little of the extreme magnitude and malignity of sin, and therefore we have only faint views of the essential goodness and holiness of God against whom sin is committed. The inviolable truth and honor of His government engage His wrath against sin. Here the sin of the world was charged upon Jesus, and exposed Him to the "reproach" of the Father, which broke His heart.

"I am full of heaviness"—In the original Hebrew the whole phrase is expressed by one word variously rendered: "I am afflicted," "I am dejected," "I faint with sickness." This began in Gethsemane where Jesus spoke clearly to His disciples saying "My soul is exceeding sorrowful even unto death" (Matt. 26:38). He entreated them to tarry there and watch with Him. When He returned the first, second and third time, He found them sleeping. They seemed unable to understand His sorrow, His deep anguish, and the drops of blood falling to the ground like sweat.

It was no impeachment of His innocence, or of His willingness, that He prayed, if it were possible, that this "cup" should pass from Him. His soul shrank from the approaching death—when it would become an offering for sin (Isa. 53:10). He was terrified, amazed and filled with indescribable consternation of mind when He suffered "in our stead." He was truly and properly a man; as a man He suffered, and He suffered alone. His suffering was peculiar to Himself in that He "tasted death for every man" (Heb. 2:9). No mere human suffering can ever portray His suffering. No human words can ever express it. No finite mind can ever comprehend it. We can only weep as we worship Him, and worship Him as we rejoice—for He has triumphed gloriously and ever liveth.

"See, from His head, His hands, His feet,
Sorrow and love flow mingled down;
Did e'er such love and sorrow meet,
Or thorns compose so rich a crown?"

–Isaac Watts

"I looked for some to take pity, but there was none, for comforters, but I found none"—Under the accumulated distress and the inconceivable anguish of soul, He looked for comforters. Among His own disciples, He was betrayed by one, denied by another and forsaken by all. It was the insensibility and inconstancy of those who professed the greatest love and attachment to Him which became one of the most bitter ingredients in the cup of His sufferings. But the most devastating of all was the silence of the Father God when Jesus prayed, "Hide not Thy face from Thy servant; for I am in trouble: hear Me speedily" (Ps. 69:17).

Forsaken thus by God and men, He drank the cup of God's wrath alone.

Lamentations 1:12

Is it nothing to you, all ye that pass by?
behold, and see if there be any sorrow
like unto my sorrow, which is done unto me,
wherewith the Lord hath afflicted me
in the day of his fierce anger.

"Is it nothing to you, all ye that pass by?"—The query in the context is quite obviously addressed to the nations and peoples who had no sympathy for the remnants of Judah, and rather enjoyed seeing their deep afflictions. But immediately the thought turns and becomes personal.

We see first the sad, majestic man of God, Jeremiah. For forty years he preached and warned of the coming

160

judgments of God; now he is an outcast of the people whom he loved and whom he served for so long.

"If there be any sorrow like unto my sorrow"—The weeping prophet here puts himself in the place of Christ, and feels the sorrow that Christ would feel. This is a cry of the broken heart. "The groans of his spirit prefigure those of Christ." His heart breaks under the sorrow of Christ. Jeremiah could have better watched and prayed with our Lord in Gethsemane than did the apostles because he himself suffered much more. This is the prophet Jeremiah speaking out of his own heart something of the sufferings which our Lord Jesus endured.

There has never been sorrow like unto the sorrow which the "Man of sorrows" vicariously endured in our behalf.

In concluding his discourse on this passage, John Newton said, "I defy history to show one, who ever made his own sufferings and death (John 12:24, 32-33) a necessary part of his original plan, and essential to his mission. This Christ did; He foresaw, foretold, declared their necessity, and voluntarily endured them."

Isaiah 53:8

He was taken from prison and from judgment:
and who shall declare his generation?
for he was cut off out of the land of the living:
for the transgressions of my people was he stricken.

"He was taken from prison and from judgment"—This is a difficult statement; without going into detail, the rendering of John Brown appears most satisfactory: "By an oppressive judgment, He was taken away." The formality of justice was observed in the trial of Jesus, while the grossest oppression was committed.

No means of self-defense was allowed. False witnesses were sought, and an unprincipled Roman judge was intimidated into yielding to the demands of the Jewish hierarchy.

"*Who shall declare His generation?*"—Adam's generations were declared in Genesis 5; who shall declare *His*? "Where is the progeny that shall carry along His line, and with it, His claims to the throne of David, 'His father after the flesh'? It expires with Him. That claim is His alone, and falls to the ground with His death" (F. C. Jennings).

All hopes are sorrowfully quenched! "But now is Christ risen from the dead" (1 Cor. 15:20) and eternal hope springs up for all the redeemed!

"*For He was cut off out of the land of the living*"—The Lord was "cut off" by His wicked oppressors. He was brought to a violent death. This corresponds to the same word that Daniel uses, when he says, "Messiah shall be cut off, but not for Himself" (9:26).

"*For the transgression of my people was He stricken*"— Who is there that discerns the inner significance of His sufferings, His short life, now cut off? He suffered and died not for His own but for the transgressions of God's people He was stricken. That stroke was inflicted upon Him not so much by man as by God!

The conclusive meaning of verse nine seems to be thus: His persecutors appointed His grave to be with the wicked; instead He was buried with the rich. Following His death, Joseph of Arimathea stepped forward, asked for the body of the Lord, and buried Him in his own unstained tomb.

*   *   *

 "Shall laugh Me to scorn"—The tenor's short recitative is hostile, the accompaniment is intense, agitated, compulsive.

"Let Him deliver Him..."—The insulting mockery is sung by the chorus, and some of the music conveys the sound of jeering laughter and scorn by a confused crowd. The fugue conveys the antagonism of the hostile crowd at the cross.

"Reproach (rebuke) hath broken my heart"—The tenor recitative is charged with harmonic tension and the melody proceeds with "utmost delicacy," as the anguish of the Sufferer is too profound for human sympathy. The extinguishing of all hope may be indicated by the near collapse of the melody in "neither found He any to comfort Him."

"If there be any sorrow like unto my sorrow"— This, Larsen calls "a halting despondent declamation." The horror and desolation of our Lord's suffering cannot be described in words. There has never been sorrow like unto the sorrow which the "Man of Sorrows" vicariously endured in our behalf.

The music in these passages is rendered with deep pathos[1]—vocals almost sobbing, accompanied by sympathizing instruments.

---

[1] Ability to express pathos effectively is one of three characteristics that makes Handel's *Messiah* a masterpiece according to Dean Ramsay.

Section 8

Messiah Arose from the Dead

Psalm 16:10
For thou wilt not leave my soul in hell;
neither wilt thou suffer thine Holy one
to see corruption.

This is admittedly a very difficult verse to interpret although it is at once obvious that it refers to the death and resurrection of Christ.
    "For Thou wilt not leave my[1] soul in hell"—The origi-

------

[1]It is needful to make a certain observation at this point. *Messiah* is not a collection of New Testament stories in which the Redeemer was active in the first person. The information about Christ in *Messiah* is presented in the oratorio by indirection. Consequently, as in Psalm 16: 10, the "My" was changed to "His."
    This is true in all other similar cases both in the New and in the Old Testament. In the change of the pronouns, the interpretation and meaning remain the same.
    The original score of *Messiah* is in the British Museum. The Library of Congress in Washington, D.C. has a copy of the original score. One of our men—Robert W. Teague—recently examined it and found that wherever the first person pronoun occurred, it was changed to the third person. This was done by Handel at the very beginning and not changed by those who followed him.

nal Hebrew word for "soul" is *nephesh,* and it occurs 754 times in the Old Testament. In the KJV it is translated "soul" 472 times, and in the other 282 places it is represented by forty-four different words such as "life," "heart," "person," etc.

"Sheol" original Hebrew for "hell," occurs fifty-five times in the Old Testament, and in the KJV it is translated "hell" twenty-seven times, "grave" twenty-six times and "pit" two times. The Septuagint renders it "mansion of the dead."

Comparing Scripture with Scripture, this seems to be the meaning: Following His death, our Lord's body was placed in Joseph's tomb, while His soul departed to Sheol into the heart of the earth where the spirits of the redeemed were "comforted" (Luke 16:25). That part of Sheol is referred to as "Abraham's bosom" (Luke 16:22). The penitent thief followed the Lord there inasmuch as the Lord said explicitly, "Today shalt thou be with Me in Paradise" (Abraham's bosom) (Luke 23:43).

At the expiration of the "three days and three nights," our Lord unlocked the Paradise portion of Sheol, and, according to Ephesians 4:7-9, He released a great multitude of captives, and in His ascension, He took with Him, as the first spoils of His victory in resurrection, these hitherto captive saints, and led them in triumph into the presence of God. In this connection, it is interesting to note that singular statement where we are told that "the graves were opened; and many bodies of the saints which slept arose, and came out of the graves after his resurrection, and went into the holy city, and appeared unto many" (Matt. 27:52-53).

"Neither wilt Thou suffer Thy Holy One to see corruption"—The soul of our Lord was reunited with His body after the three days and three nights. That holy body of our dear Lord was not allowed to be touched by corruption.

"Since Jesus is mine, I'll not fear undressing,
But gladly put off these garments of clay;
To die in the Lord is a covenant blessing,
Since Jesus to glory through death leads the way."

Christ's resurrection is the cause, the earnest, the guarantee, and the sure token of the resurrection of all who believe on Him!

Psalm 24:7-10

Lift up your head, O ye gates;
and be ye lift up, ye everlasting doors;
and the King of glory shall come in.

Who is this King of glory?
The Lord strong and mighty,
The Lord mighty in battle.

Lift up your heads, O ye gates;
even lift them up, ye everlasting doors;
and the King of glory shall come in.

Who is this King of glory?
The Lord of hosts,
he is the King of glory. Selah.

"Lift up your heads, O ye gates ... everlasting doors" — According to ancient English custom, when the king of England wishes to enter the city of London through Temple Bar, the herald demands entrance at the closed gate by calling, "Open the gate." From within a voice is heard, "Who is there?" The herald answers, "The King of England!" The gate is opened at once, and the king proceeds amidst the joyful acclamations of his people.

These verses picture the scene, when, after spoiling the powers of darkness, after abolishing death itself, the resurrected God-man, the Lord returns to heaven in triumph, and as He approaches the heavenly portals, the celestial herald cries out, "Lift up your heads

O ye gates, and be ye lift up, ye everlasting doors; and the King of glory shall come in." The angelic watchers within ask, "Who is this King of glory?" The answer: "The Lord strong and mighty, the Lord mighty in battle."

The redeemed of God know something of the might of the Lord, the battles which He fought and the victories He has won over sin, over death, over hell, and they rejoice as He leads the liberated saints into the presence of God.

"We conceive of Him, therefore, from this sublime passage, as ascending to His Father and our Father, to His God and our God, accompanied with a train of worshipping angels, who demand admittance for Messiah, the Savior and friend of sinners, the King of glory" (John Newton).

Might not these verses also picture a second triumphal entry into Jerusalem at the start of the millennium?

"Lift up your heads . . ."—The words are repeated with a pleasing variation. The reenactment of the scene lends force and meaning. The gates lift up, the doors swing wide open, and "the Lord strong and mighty," "the Lord mighty in battle," the Captain of our salvation, "the Lord of hosts," "the King of glory" enters amidst the joyful acclamations of heaven.

"The Lord of hosts, He is the King of glory"—Christ is the Jehovah of armies. He has authority over all the heavenly hosts.

The bringing of the ark into the city of David was but a faint shadow of our Lord's ascension to heaven.

There are those who interpret this passage as a description of the Lord's triumph on His return to earth. The long-awaited Messiah, the Lord "strong" and "mighty in battle" shall return to crush the proud, opposing nations and deliver His earthly people Israel.

Hebrews 1:5

For unto which of the angels
said he at any time,
Thou art my Son,
this day have I begotten thee?
And again,
I will be to him a Father,
and he shall be to me a Son?

The indisputable answer to both questions asked in this verse is—*to none of them.*

"Thou art my Son, this day have I begotten thee"—This is a quotation from Psalm 2, which is, of course, a reference to Christ. From the unbeginning ages of eternity past, Christ was the Son begotten by the Father. The words must, therefore, be understood, not of His being *constituted* as the eternal Son, but simply as a *declaration* of His eternal Sonship. The words are equivalent to saying, "I proclaim You my Son—My begotten Son." This could be correctly *declared* at *any* day—in the past, in the present, or in the future.

"Begotten" speaks of the eternal generation of the Son by God the Father. This is a difficult concept because it reaches into eternal things, many of which go beyond human comprehension.

"I will be to Him a Father, and He shall be to Me a Son"— Taken from 2 Samuel 7:14, this is a prophecy of the Messiah.

Hebrews 1:6

And again,
when he bringeth in the first begotten
into the world,
he saith,
And let all the angels of God
worship him.

This is a difficult verse. It is a direct quotation of Deuteronomy 32:43 from the Septuagint version. The substance of it may also be gathered from Psalm 97. Kenneth Wuest in his expanded translation has it: "And whenever He shall have brought again the first-born into the inhabited earth, He saith, And let all the angels of God worship Him."

"Let all the angels of God worship Him"—Messiah's superiority to angels is seen in the fact that angels are commanded to worship Him.

Psalm 68:18

Thou hast ascended on high,
thou hast led captivity captive:
thou hast received gifts for men;
yea for the rebellious also,
that the Lord God might dwell among them.

"Thou hast ascended on high, Thou hast led captivity captive"—This is quoted by the apostle Paul in Ephesians chapter 4. Christ ascended to heaven with a great company of saints who had been held captive in Sheol. This has been expounded at some length in connection with Psalm 16:10.

In Roman times, the returning conquering general would parade through the city in triumph, followed by his captives, his trophies. A similar scene is portrayed here as believers, the trophies of His grace, follow after Christ.

"Thou has received gifts for men; yea for the rebellious also"—The supreme gift for believers was the Holy Spirit, who came down to indwell believers following the Lord's ascension (Acts 2:4, 33). Other "gifts" with which the Lord enriches the body of Christ are "evangelists, pastors and teachers" (Eph. 4:11). Rebels among us are conquered by His love, and become

"captives" of the One who "loved us and gave Himself for us."

"That the Lord God might dwell among them"—When the Lord God, in all the glory of His holy name, conquers the hearts of rebellious men, He makes them His living temples.

> "Great King of grace my heart subdue
> I would be led in triumph too
> A willing captive to my Lord
> To own the conquest of His Word."

* * *

"Thou didst not leave My soul in hell . . ."—Supernatural business of the highest order is taking place, and the soprano (sometimes a tenor) in a high range relates the facts in a somber way.

Some biographers fail to comprehend the fact that Christ is the subject of many Old Testament prophecies, and they have difficulty in seeing how Psalm 16:10 refers specifically to the resurrection of Christ.

The key change signals the introduction of hope; the Messiah's death is not the end of the story!

"Lift up your heads . . . The Lord of hosts: He is the King of glory"—The chorus, in a joyous, jubilant manner, sings of our Lord's triumph over death and the grave in a coronation anthem style. This chorus has a mixture of homophonic and polyphonic music, very typical of Handel.

"The chorus begins without instruments and is performed excellently by such fine number of bass and tenor voices in unison. The contrast of sensation occasioned by the harmony and activity of the several parts afterwards make for a striking effect" (Charles Burney).

"Lift up your heads": The male and female voices take turns asking the question, "Who is the King of glory?" They continue to alternate in giving the answer—"The Lord strong and mighty, the Lord mighty in battle." The voices join in the declaration, "The LORD of Hosts, He is the King of glory!" The gladness of this chorus images the celebration of a conquering monarch.

(Two verses in this section are frequently omitted in the performance of *Messiah*.)

"Let all the angels worship Him . . ."—The chorus again comes on exultingly, and angels are called upon to worship the One who has conquered death and the grave.

"Thou art gone on high . . ."—The accompaniment to the soprano is joyous and spirited.

One of the striking features of Handel's wisdom and tact, as various music critics notice, is not to overlay his choruses with heavy instrumental accompaniments, as some have done since. Handel excels highly in one of the most exalted departments of human attainments.

Section 9

Messiah Proclaimed

Psalm 68:11
The Lord gave the word:
great was the company of those
that published it.

Maclaren described verses 11-14 in this Psalm as "the despair of commentators."

"The Lord gave the word"—It is the sovereign word of *power* as in Psalm 33:9—"He spake and it was done." This word of power not only commands the war and promises the victory, but effects the victory. By His word of power the enemies of Israel were discomfited.

"Great was the company of those that published it"—"Company" refers to an army or host. The word "those" is feminine. Literally it means, "great was the company of women that published it." If the "word" was a command of God as to an approaching enemy, the women, great in number, ran from tent to tent in arousing the valiant men for battle. This is the interpretation of C. H. Spurgeon. "Those" could refer to the songs of victory proclaimed by women as Miriam did at the Red Sea.

The verse is often used with the meaning as it appears on the surface. God gave us His Word, and the company of those that "publish" it includes printers, publishers, preachers, teachers, missionaries, writers and all of God's true witnesses.

Romans 10:15

**And how shall they preach,
except they be sent?
as it is written,
How beautiful are the feet of them
that preach the gospel of peace,
and bring glad tidings of good things!**

"And how shall they preach, except they be sent?"—It is God who calls. It is God who "sends." God initiates the preaching of the gospel.

"How beautiful are the feet of them that preach the gospel of peace"—The real beauty is not so much in the feet of the messengers as it is in the loveliness and gladness of the message which is presented by the eager feet that "spring over the mountain with all the swiftness of gazelles." "Behold upon the mountains the feet of him that bringeth good tidings, that publisheth peace" (Nahum 1:15).

In 2 Samuel 18:24-29, we have a graphic illustration of a runner. King David is anxiously awaiting the news concerning the battle where his rebellious son Absalom was involved—"Behold a man running alone . . . Behold another man running alone." The king yearns to hear good news.

The example of the deep appreciation that is felt for the messengers is the way the Galatians felt about Paul. He preached, and they heard, they believed and they rejoiced. The apostle reminds them, that they had not received a cold speculative doctrine, but such as imparted "blessedness" to them. For a time the personal knowledge of a Savior made them exceedingly joyful, and while they were so, they felt strong emotions of gratitude and esteem for the messenger who brought them these glad tidings. They received him as "an angel of God," and gave him every testimony of the most cordial friendship; insomuch, that, had it been possible, they would have plucked out their own eyes, and would have given them to him (Gal. 4:15).

"*Gospel of peace*" (good news)—It is a peace *with* God (Rom. 5:1); it is a peace that passes understanding (Phil. 4:7). It brings blessed assurance of salvation. Those who believe the "report" of the gospel (Isa. 53:1) and experience all the blessedness that the "arm of the Lord" reveals, derive from it peace of conscience, which dispels all fear.

"*Glad tidings of good things*"—The gospel of peace proposes a cordial for every care, a balm for every wound. No one who takes advantage of its efficacy is ever disappointed; instead, he revels in the unebbing stream of "good things" that flow from it.

How appropriate, how fitting it is that these "words" (taken from Romans 10, but originally spoken in Isaiah 52:7) should come here immediately preceding the chapter where Isaiah presents the greatest and most complete prophecy of the Messiah in all the Old Testament (Isaiah 53). In the judgment of some, this chapter exceeds the record of our Lord's sufferings in the New Testament.

Romans 10:18

But I say, Have they not heard?
Yes verily,
their sound went into all the earth,
and their words
unto the ends of the world.

"But I say, Have they not heard?"—Is the faculty of hearing wanting? Is there a lack of spiritual perception?

"Verily, their sound went into all the earth"—God has revealed Himself to the peoples of the whole world from the beginning, if not by the preaching of men, yet by the witness of His creation (Ps. 19:3-4).

"The grandeur of the arch over our heads, the number and lustre of the stars, the beauty of the light, the splendor of the sun, the regular succession of day and night, and of the seasons of the year, are such proofs of infinite wisdom and power, that Scripture attributes to them a voice, a universal language, intelligible to all mankind, accommodated to every capacity. There is no speech nor language where their voice is not heard" (John Newton).

The combined effect of the visible works of the supreme Architect (Ps. 19), presses a declaration upon the ear of right reason—"The hand that made us is divine" (Joseph Addison). But the loudest voice is unnoticed by the spiritually deaf; the bulk of mankind is no more affected by the wondrous works of God than are the beasts of the field—probably less so.

Though the evidence does not excite admiration and praise of God, it is abundantly sufficient to convict man of ingratitude and unbelief, and to leave him without excuse (Rom. 1:20).

* * *

"Great was the company . . ." The company of marching evangelists is here portrayed. The trumpet fanfare style reverberates throughout this chorus.

"How beautiful are the feet. . ." The chorus begins in a delightful flowing rhythm depicting meditation upon the sweetness of the message they bring. This is followed by a more lively tendency.

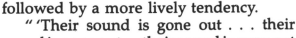 " 'Their sound is gone out . . . their sound is gone out ... their sound is gone out ... their sound is gone out ...' "—Soprano, alto, tenor, bass: one voice line after another picks up the theme as the chorus sings of the messengers' destination. There is an expansive sweep to the line 'and their words unto the ends of the world' that suggests the sun in Psalm 19, running its course with joy from one end of the earth to the other" (Roger A. Bullard).

John S. Dwight, author of the great Christmas hymn, "O Holy Night," points out that Handel's melodies are all different: "No two of them are flowers which go by the same name or exude the same fragrance."

Section 10

Messiah Repulsed

Psalm 2:1-3

**Why do the heathen rage,
and the people imagine a vain thing?**

**The kings of the earth set themselves,
and the rulers take counsel together,
against the Lord, and against his anointed,
saying,**

**Let us break their bands asunder,
and cast away their cords from us.**

This is a Messianic Psalm. It is quoted seven times in the New Testament.

In the first three verses we have an account of man's perennial hatred toward the Lord Jesus Christ, as the representative of God's sovereignty.

"Why do the people rage . . .?"—The fury and rage of the heathen were roaring like the restless sea against the Lord of glory. Their folly is motivated by their deep-seated wickedness. History is filled with the sad accounts of enmity against Christ.

"The kings of the earth set themselves together . . ."—Kings and rulers confederate and plot wicked schemes

176

against God and against His anointed, the Messiah. Wickedness and rebellion pervade their thoughts.

"Let us break their bands asunder, and cast away their cords from us"—They protest that they have been too restricted. The objective of their plotting is seen here. Let us have our own gods! Let us be free to do as we desire! Let us get rid of all restraints! They will not have the Christ of God to rule over them. Fallen man ever clings to the usurper's sway and resists the rule of God in his heart. "We will not have this man to reign over us" (Lu. 19:14).

This opposition to God reached its climax when the rulers and religious leaders crucified the sinless Son of God. Our Lord's parable in Matthew 21:33-42 illustrates the truth of this Psalm.

This part of the Psalm has been literally fulfilled and it is quoted by the apostle in Acts 4:23-28.

Psalm 2:4

**He that sitteth in the heavens
shall laugh:
the Lord shall have them in derision.**

The camera shifts from earth to heaven, showing God the Father unmoved by the puny rebellion of man. We note the full assurance and the quiet dignity of the most high God. The powers of wickedness in our eyes are formidable and often frightening, but they are insignificant and despicable in the estimation of God. He actually holds them in contempt. "Laugh" and "derision" are terms ascribed to God for the sake of our understanding. Actually God is incapable of any vain passions.

The unbelieving Jews and Gentiles sent Jesus Christ back to heaven with this label: "We will not have this man to reign over us" (Lu. 19:14). But God declares, "Yet have I set my king upon my holy hill of Zion" (Ps. 2:6).

In verse seven we witness an unusual scene.

Throughout the New Testament we read of how the Father says, "This is my beloved Son in whom I am well pleased." But here in Psalm 2:7, the Lord Christ says, "I will declare the decree: the Lord [Jehovah] hath said unto Me, Thou art My Son, this day have I begotten Thee." This is likely a reference to His resurrection.

"Ask of Me," the Father says to the Son, "and I will give Thee the heathen for thine inheritance, and the uttermost parts of the earth for Thy possession." The rule of Christ will ultimately be worldwide.

Psalm 2:9

**Thou shalt break them
with a rod of iron;
thou shalt dash them in pieces
like a potter's vessel.**

The silent contempt of God for His foes and their wicked plots shall continue until the time chosen by Him for the display of His power and justice. Then "He shall speak to them in His wrath, and vex them in His sore displeasure" (2:5).

Because all power is given to Christ to execute vengeance on the unreconciled, the Father says to Him, "Thou shalt break them with a rod of iron, Thou shalt dash them in pieces like a potter's vessel." Before our Lord enters His reign of righteousness, He must first break His enemies and establish His supremacy.

We read of our Lord's judgment and destruction of the nations in the end time in Revelation 19:11-16: "And I saw heaven opened, and behold a white horse, and He that sat upon him was called Faithful and True, and in righteousness He doth judge and make war . . .

And the armies which were in heaven followed Him upon white horses, clothed in fine linen, white and clean. And out of His mouth goeth a sharp sword, that with it He should smite the nations, and He shall rule them with a rod of iron; and He treadeth the winepress of the fierceness and wrath of Almighty God. And He hath on His vesture and on His thigh a name written, KING OF KINGS, AND LORD OF LORDS."

"Kiss the Son, lest He be angry, and ye perish from the way, when His wrath is kindled but a little (2:12). Give reverence to the "heir apparent."

"Blessed are all they that put their trust in Him" (2:12).

"Ye sinners seek His grace whose wrath you cannot bear;
Fly to the shadow of the cross, and find salvation there."

* * *

The musical character of this section, though suited well to the words, is so different from all the rest, that at first it seems to threaten the unity of the entire composition. "The leaping motion at the beginning of the two main motives is particularly noticeable" (Larsen).

"Why do the heathen [nations] rage..." asks the angry bass solo with operatic power; the harshness of the melody and rhythm become at once apparent. The vain rage of the heathen is flouted in the turbulent energy of the bass air. The vigorous bass voice also portrays the strife of a battlefield with his question, "Why do the nations rage so furiously together?"

"Let us break their bands asunder . . ." In this "crowd" chorus, the words are flung out from all sides, and the two themes seem to chase each other vigorously. All this creates tension and propels us forward—"He . . . shall laugh." The rapid fugue suggests the voices of a war-like, rebellious multitude.

"Thou shalt break them with a rod of iron"—God's wrath is provoked by the rebellion and defiance of man. The tenor aria with an aroused, angry accompaniment vividly depicts the reduction of proud kingdoms to an expanse of broken earthenware.

The thunderous "rage-aria" becomes almost a full-blown coloratura on certain words, including "rage," "imagine," "break" and "potter's."

Section 11

The Hallelujah of the Redeemed

Revelation 19:6

**And I heard as it were
the voice of a great multitude,
and as the voice of many waters,
and as the voice of mighty thunderings,
saying, Hallelujah:
for the Lord God omnipotent reigneth.**

The verse before us will have little meaning unless we take note, at least briefly, of what happened in the two chapters preceding chapter nineteen of Revelation. Careful and patient attention here is necessary.

In Revelation chapter seventeen is recorded the fall of ecclesiastical Babylon—a powerful worldwide religious organization. This great ecclesiastical multinational conglomerate is spoken of as "the great whore that sitteth upon many waters: with whom the kings of the earth have committed fornication . . . The woman was arrayed in purple and scarlet color, and decked with gold and precious stones and pearls, having a golden cup in her hand, full of abominations and filthi-

181

ness of her fornication: And upon her forehead was a name written: MYSTERY, BABYLON THE GREAT, THE MOTHER OF HARLOTS AND ABOMINATIONS OF THE EARTH."

"'And I saw," continues the apostle John, "the woman drunken with the blood of saints, and with the blood of martyrs of Jesus":

Suddenly the judgment of God falls upon ecclesiastical Babylon: And another angel cried: "Babylon the great is fallen, is fallen, and is become the habitation of devils . . ." (Rev. 18:2).

The ecclesiastical Babylon had close affinity with the kings and rulers of the whole world, and wielded great political power. "In ecclesiastical form, Babylon is the foe of Christ's true Church: in political form, she is the foe of Christ's kingdom" (Ford C. Ottman).

The leadership of the whole world was enamored with the bewitching schemes and the enriching power of the ecclesiastical "harlot." The record in Revelation chapter eighteen speaks of their reactions: "The kings of the earth" mourn and lament (vs. 9); "the merchants of the earth" are full of tears and grief over her sudden collapse (vs. 11). Alas, alas, woe, woe is the wail from warehouses and homes throughout the world!

But who and what is this "ecclesiastical Babylon"? Read your Bible, read your history and you will surely begin to understand. "Babylon is the fountainhead of all idolatry and systems of false worship. This is the 'mystery of iniquity' (2 Thess. 2:7) seen in all the great 'religions' of the world. All alike substitute another god for the God of the Bible—a religion consisting of human merit and endeavor" (E. W. Bullinger). Read your news periodicals and see how quickly the world church is forming. The liberal wise men and communicators are highly impressed by the mighty ecclesiastical power while condescendingly—and sometimes ungraciously—tolerating those who take their Bibles seriously.

But while lamentation and terror fill the whole earth, a holy jubilation fills the heavens: "Rejoice over her, thou heaven, and ye holy apostles and prophets; for God hath avenged you on her" (Rev. 18:20).

The whole present world system, in the paw of Satan, has been against the true faith and testimony of the saints, apostles and prophets for 6,000 years. The faith and testimonies of the servants of God appear to the natural man as mere hallucinations.

The ecclesiastical harlot has had her day; suddenly night falls upon her without any star of hope. She has lured, deluded and debauched the world because fallen men preferred her abominations to the solid, eternal truth of God.

Now that the false church and the kingdom of Satan, which are one and the same, have been judged by God Himself, the sublime outbursts of the true servants of God begin.

In the first six verses of chapter nineteen there are four boundless "Alleluias."

The word "Alleluia" occurs twenty-four times in the book of Psalms, but it is spelled "Hallelujah." It is one Hebrew word which means "praise Jehovah" or "praise the Lord"—from *halelu*, praise, and *Jah*, a short form for Jehovah.

The Geneva Bible in the 1602 edition has it "Hallelujah," and it would have been preferable in all translations. "Alleluia" crept into English through the transliteration of the Greek. The Greek expresses the "H" with a breathing mark rather than a letter and the sound of this breathing mark is lost in many translations. It is good that Handel chose to use the full "Hallelujah" in *Messiah* because it is certainly more singable and seems more forceful than "Alleluia."

Anselm, Archbishop of Canterbury (1033-1109) considered "Hallelujah" to be a divine, angelic word, which cannot be fully reproduced by one word in any language, and concurred with Augustine of Hippo (354-430) that the "feeling and saying of it embodies all the blessedness of heaven." Hallelujah!

Dr. John F. Elliott believes that when "Paul was caught up to the third heaven, he saw things there which he was not allowed to utter, but later—at the appropriate time—the apostle John saw the same things and was allowed to write what Paul probably had already seen." No one can be certain of this, but it is a fascinating conjecture.

J. A. Seiss, one of the most creditable expositors of Revelation (Kregel Publishers), writes concerning "Hallelujah." "It is one of the very highest acknowledgements and celebrations of God. Where it is understandingly sung, there is at once the profoundest adoration and the most exultant joy. And this is the feeling and experience in the heaven when the proud system of this world's apostate wisdom and glory falls."

"Loud as from numbers without number,
Sweet as from blest voices uttering joy."

Now, back to Revelation 19:6. First the two preceding verses: "And the four and twenty elders and the four living creatures fell down and worshipped God that sat on the throne, saying, Amen; Hallelujah. And a voice came out of the throne, saying, Praise our God, all ye His servants, and ye that fear the Lord, both small and great."

"*Voice of a great multitude . . .*" (Rev. 19:6)—This represents inconceivable volume. The sound of "many waters" suggests *cataracts*, and the "mighty thunders" are gigantic reverberations. Both of these similes portray the boundlessness of the chorus of God's praise.

"For the Lord God omnipotent reigneth"—The judgment of Great Babylon has taken place, and the Lord God omnipotent reigneth! His scepter is now over all. The government is now "upon His shoulder," as Isaiah foretold (9:6).

Revelation 11:15

And the seventh angel sounded;
and there were great voices in heaven,
saying,
The kingdoms of this world
are become the kingdoms of our Lord,
and of His Christ;
and He shall reign for ever and ever.

"And the seventh angel sounded"—The seventh angel's trumpet brings us to the portals of the new creation in Revelation 21. All heaven has long anticipated this moment. It would seem right to expect the seventh trumpet to reveal the act of final judgment or some part of it. But instead something greater is offered —a scene in heaven—*after* the judgment. Here is the climax of the preceding six trumpets. Although the Scripture before us describes a scene in heaven, it also marks the beginning of the millennium on earth where the King of Kings begins His reign on David's throne.

R. C. H. Lenski, a great Lutheran scholar whose monumental twelve volumes on the entire New Testament have been a help to many students, offers a perceptive comment: "It has been well observed that there is a certain similarity in the seventh seal, the seventh trumpet and the seventh bowl (16:17, etc.); all three of these sevens begin in a most majestic way with voices in heaven; all three place us most plainly at the end. Those are undoubtedly right who perceive that these three series of sevens are not consecutive, are not twenty-one successive chapters in history of the world or of the church on earth, but that each group of sevens takes us over the same ground and shows us three groups of parallel scenes, each group in its seventh member taking us to the end."

It might be appropriate at this point to recognize that the details in the book of Revelation reach far out into eternity, and that it is virtually impossible to comprehend the meaning of them all accurately, though some appear to think they can. One should be content to remain ignorant of some of these things which will be made perfectly clear in heaven. Nor should this discourage anyone from searching diligently (1 Peter 1:10-12) these Scriptures under the illumination of the ever-present blessed Holy Spirit, who "searcheth all things, yea, the deep things of God" (1 Cor. 2:10).

The Scripture before us tells us plainly that "the kingdoms of this world" are "become the kingdoms of our Lord," and "He shall reign for ever and ever." All the wars, all the problems—economical, political, environmental—will come under the suzerainty of the perfect King, the world's long anticipated omnipotent, benevolent Dictator.

Handel is to be commended for recognizing that Revelation 11:15 is in perfect accord with Revelation 19:6, which we have already studied.

Dr. Francis A. Schaeffer in his discerning book on *How Shall We Then Live*, places Handel's *Messiah* in the tradition of restored Christianity which came about through John Huss, Martin Luther and others. Schaeffer goes on to say that "The *Messiah* could only have come forth in a setting where the Bible stood at the center . . . For example, Handel did not put the 'Hallelujah Chorus' at the end, but in its proper place in the flow of the past and future history of Christ."

In the Reformation there was strong desire for a simplified style of worship where the words would be understood. "In England as in Germany the stress was on content. Music was not incidental to the Reformation's return to biblical teaching; it was a natural outcome, a unity with what the Bible taught" (Schaeffer).

Revelation 19:16

**And He hath on His vesture
and on His thigh a name written,
KING OF KINGS, AND LORD OF LORDS.**

"And He hath on His vesture and on His thigh . . ."—Understanding exactly where the Lord's title was written is difficult. It has been suggested that His title was written on a sign which hung over the vesture (mantle), not partly on the mantle and partly on the skin of the thigh—an unsatisfactory supposition.

The Psalmist in anticipation said, "Gird Thy sword upon Thy thigh, O most Mighty" (45:3). Normally the warrior carried his sword upon his thigh, but here the "sharp sword" proceeds "out of the Lord's mouth" (Rev. 19:15). On the thigh His name is written—the name of His absolute authority and power. All the forces of men confederated with Hell itself will fall like the seed of dandelions before the forces of Omnipotence. "The Lord shall swallow them up in His wrath, and the fire shall devour them" (Ps. 21:9).

"KING OF KINGS AND LORD OF LORDS"—This is our Lord's official title. It belongs to Him as the Son of man, the rightful heir of all things, and the only possible heir to the everlasting throne of David. When He came the first time, He was mocked with the crown of thorns; now He is exalted and extolled above all. The kingdoms of the whole earth are His, and He will rule the nations with the rod of iron in unmitigated justice.

This is the final and complete fulfillment of Psalm 2; "The kings of the earth set themselves, and the rulers take counsel together, against the Lord ... He that sitteth in the heavens shall laugh: the Lord shall have them in derision. Then shall He speak unto them in His wrath, and vex them in His sore displeasure. Yet have I set My king upon My holy hill of Zion" (Ps. 2: 2-6).

"The Hallelujah Chorus is not just an anthem chorus having no specific characterization. It is one of those frame choruses fulfilling two functions: as an integrating part of the greater whole, and as a relatively self-contained, anthem-like final reflection. Only against the background of the preceding apostasy, of the revolt against Almighty God, does the position of the Hallelujah Chorus become clear. It is not merely an obligatory finale, but a settlement of the preceding conflict between God and man" (Jens Peter Larsen).

Not until after the announcement of the Lord's supreme dominion can discord be completely and permanently resolved: The kingdoms of this world are become the Kingdom of our Lord.

* * *

"Hallelujah . . ."—Praise the Lord! We hear, we feel, we delight in the music of the Redeemer's glorious triumph.

So often this chorus is heard out of its context. When heard after the preceding four songs of warfare, the Hallelujah Chorus becomes the diadem of praise for the conquering King.

"All the energy so far contained, all the emotions so far restrained, are here released in an explosion of choral splendor. It is a moment all participants and auditors await, when Handel shows himself the master of form. He takes simple melody and straightforward, anthem-like rhythm, and through splits of voices and irrepressible repetitions intensifies the expression of joy, of triumph, of a king enthroned... We seem to see the glory, the majesty swelling to the heavens. Triumph achieved" (Peter Jacobi).

"The primary impression of the chorus is powerful simplicity and plentiful life. The simplicity so characteristic of Handel's style in general, is apparent throughout in the shape of the themes, the harmony, the tonality, the orchestration, and above all in the general conception of the chorus . . .

"The basic motive 'Hallelujah' and its complementary 'for ever,' enclose, encircle and oppose the whole series of quietly sustained themes. Handel has nowhere surpassed the effect of firmness coupled with freedom, restriction with boundlessness, than this chorus achieves" (Jens Peter Larsen).

Charles Burney, who attended that splendid performance of *Messiah* at Westminster Abbey in 1784, made some engaging comments: " 'And He shall reign forever and forever' is the most pleasing and fertile fugue that has ever been invented since the art of the fugue was cultivated... The words 'KING OF KINGS AND LORD OF LORDS,' always set to a single sound which seems to stand at bay while the others attack it in every possible manner."

This superlative chorus in its entirety keeps the believer in Messiah on the cutting edge of pure spiritual exultation!

Section 12

The Expectation
of the Redeemed

The pinnacle was reached with the Hallelujah Chorus, but there is more. Although the Redeemer's triumph was wonderfully achieved in that chorus, the total victory of those for whom He suffered and died has not yet been attained.

To conclude the oratorio at this point would be comparable to what appears to be the unfinished part of Milton's *Paradise Regained*. There are scholars who believe that *Paradise Regained* falls short of what one would naturally expect. Far-reaching questions and problems raised in *Paradise Lost* are not fully answered in the four books of *Paradise Regained*. Indeed, our Lord gained the full victory as is so effectively written in the four books, but the state of those for whom Christ died seems not to be fully addressed.

Job 19:25-26

For I know that my Redeemer liveth,
and that He shall stand
at the latter day
upon the earth:

190

And though after my skin
worms destroy this body,
yet in my flesh shall I see God:

Following the moving, dramatic music of the Hallelujahs comes the sweet soprano air, "I know that my Redeemer liveth."

"I know that my Redeemer liveth"—Surrounded by his three miserable comforters—and Satan with them—and overwhelmed by the darkness and sorrows of the hour, Job suddenly catches the music of eternal things, as it swept across the strings which were stretched almost to the breaking point by suffering. Although Job did not likely conceive the full meaning of the incarnation, nevertheless, by faith he somehow perceived the day when his Redeemer would visit the earth.

Job had previously declared that His Witness and Recorder was in heaven (16:19), and now he gives that Witness the name "Redeemer."

The Hebrew word for "Redeemer" here is the important term "Goel." The Goel is the kinsman-redeemer—the nearest and next of kin—who would defend the cause and avenge wrongs done to the one deceased. In the midst of his agony, for a moment at least, Job was convinced that while there was no one to stand for him in this life, yet he had a Kinsman who was his Advocate, the One through Whom he would be acquitted.

"He shall stand at the latter day upon the earth"—By faith Job saw more: he envisioned Christ standing upon the earth in the end times.

"Yet in my flesh shall I see God"—Here Job's faith sees remarkably far into the future. Though his body would be destroyed by worms, as are others, yet, in an incorruptible body, he confidently anticipated seeing

God. This expectation is inspiringly conveyed by the music in *Messiah*.

1 Corinthians 15:20

But now is Christ risen
from the dead,
and become the firstfruits
of them that slept.

"But now has Christ risen from the dead"—The words "but now" introduce an emphatic change from the preceding negative discussion (1 Cor. 15:13-19) to the triumphant announcement of the positive fact of Christ's resurrection. We know that He who died has been raised up. He Himself said, "I lay down my life, that I may take it again." He was put to death in the flesh but quickened by the Spirit. "The God of peace ... brought again from the dead our Lord Jesus, that great Shepherd of the sheep (Heb. 13:20).

"Become the firstfruits of them that slept"—This is an allusion to Leviticus 23:11: On the day following the Passover Sabbath, the first sheaf of the new crop was presented in the temple, with a sacrifice. It was an acknowledgement that all came from God, and that His part should first be given to Him. Christ's resurrection is the solid token of our resurrection as believers. Christ will not remain alone in the state of glory. Godet: "Christ risen is to the multitude of believers who shall rise again at His Advent what a first ripe ear, gathered by hand, is to the whole harvest."

1 Corinthians 15:21-22

For since by man came death,
by man came also
the resurrection of the dead.

For as in Adam all die,
even so in Christ
shall all be made alive.

"Since by man came death, by man came also the resurrection of the dead"—The human origin of these two opposite phases in the existence of humanity is set in relief. By Adam's disobedience (and ours with him) subjection to death was imposed on men. Through man there must come to them the power of rising again.

"In Adam all die . . . in Christ shall all be made alive"— "For as by one man's disobedience many were made sinners, so by the obedience of one shall many be made righteous" (Rom. 5:19). "As Adam is the head of the natural race, and, in virtue of this natural relation with him, death is the common lot of men, so by reason of the fact that Christ is the Head of the spiritual, all who possess spiritual relation with Him will be made alive. There is no idea of the universalism of the human race in this comparison of the second statement with the first. That unbelievers are 'In Christ' is utterly contrary to the teaching of Scripture" (W. E. Vine).

*　*　*

 In an appropriate choice of Scripture and an equally brilliant stroke of music, Part 3 opens with the words from Job: "I know that my Redeemer liveth . . ."— "This ineffably beautiful aria," Lang observes, "is sheer transfigured enchantment." This is an apt observation concerning the music, but for the believer the reassuring words spoken by God's "trial-piece" expressed

in such appropriate music brings sheer transforming exhilaration!

Handel knew his English Bible well and was inspiringly able to craft the matchless music for the timeless words.

In each instrumental interlude in "I know that my Redeemer liveth," the swell of the violins in recapitulating the melody, not only brings support for the soprano, but, verily, it enraptures the believer in Messiah with ineffable, inexpressible delight.

One would love to have been able to hear this lovely melody sung by Jenny Lind—in her incomparable range, modulation and control—as the people in Halle, Germany, heard it in 1857 at the dedication of a statue of Handel.

"But now is Christ risen from the dead . . . so in Christ shall all be made alive."

When the soprano climbs magnificently to the upper G note, with full, pleasing volume on the word "risen," one feels the thrust of that clear sound sweeping swiftly toward heaven and bearing the listener with it. Only the "dead" must be unimpressed and unawakened by its intrinsic power.

The soft, gentle solo tells of Christ's resurrection, and the chorus makes application of it to all the redeemed in a joyously exploding *allegro* (lively movement) concerning resurrection life.

Larsen sees in this lovely melody Handel's indebtedness to the English spirit, and how remarkable it is that Handel's music has now been recognized for some two and a half centuries as a true expression of that spirit.

"Since by man came death"—The soft, doleful tones on "Since by man came death," suddenly give way to the loud, joyous announcement, "By man came also the resurrection of the dead."

Section 13

The Transformation of the Redeemed

1 Corinthians 15:51-52

Behold, I show you a mystery;
We shall not all sleep,
but we shall all be changed,

In a moment, in the twinkling of an eye,
at the last trump:
for the trumpet shall sound,
and the dead shall be raised incorruptible,
and we shall be changed.

"*Behold, I show you a mystery*"—Not something mysterious as such. The reference to mystery pertains to the revelation of a hitherto unrevealed purpose of God.

"*We shall not all sleep, but we shall all be changed*"— We shall not all die; there will be Christians living in the natural body when the Lord comes again. But all— the living Christians and the dead Christians—must be changed: living believers by transformation, the dead believers by resurrection into incorruptible

195

bodies. It is impossible to enter heaven in the earthly body which is composed of materials subject to corruption. Corruption cannot inherit incorruption.

"In a moment, in the twinkling of an eye"—This marks the swiftness and the suddenness of the event. No signs, no warnings!

G. Campbell Morgan (1863-1945) said, "I never begin my work in the morning without thinking that perhaps the Lord may interrupt my work and lift me to glory. I am not looking for death. I am looking for Him (Titus 2:13-14)."

"At the last trump"—This is a description of a divine signal, the nature of which we do not know. In 1 Thessalonians 4:16, the signal is called, "the voice of an archangel, and with the trump of God."

> The trumpet! The trumpet! dead Christians
>   have heard:
> Lo, the depths of stone-cover'd charnels
>   are stirr'd.
> From the sea, from the land,
>   from the south, from the north,
> The vast generations of man
>   are come forth.   —Milman

Imagine reading this when it has been reported all over the world that millions of people suddenly disappeared. Some reported seeing people getting out of the graves and rising into the air in beautiful, radiant bodies!

"Well, so what?"

Well it just means that you missed it, because all believers in Christ—dead and alive—were caught up to meet the Lord in the air.

"What? what? what can I do?" you say.

Receive the Lord Jesus Christ as Savior right now (Jn. 1:12-13), and God will take care of you.

"The dead shall be raised incorruptible"—The bodies of dead believers will be raised first (1 Thess. 4:16). The fact that they died places them at no disadvantage. There is an order mentioned but no interval of time between them. The resurrection of the unsaved is not in view here at all. It will take place after a long interval (Rev. 20:5).

"And we shall be changed"—The thought seems to be that the "change" in the case of the living believers will result in the same kind of glorified body as in the case of those who are raised from the dead.

1 Corinthians 15:54

So when this corruptible
shall have put on incorruption,
and this mortal
shall have put on immortality,
then shall be brought to pass
the saying that is written,
Death is swallowed up in victory.

" . . . must put on incorruption . . . immortality"—The "must" predicates the absolute necessity of the change. This confirms what was told in 1 Corinthians 15:42-44. For believers who have died, "incorruption" is that state of body attained through resurrection. An incorruptible body is one not subject to death and decay produced by the Fall. For believers still living at Christ's return, "immortality" is attained by an immediate change, apart from death. The final result is identical. This is made clear in other Scriptures: "For our conversation [citizenship] is in heaven; from whence also we look for the Savior, the Lord Jesus Christ: who shall change our vile body [body of humiliation], that it may be fashioned like unto His glorious body, according to the working whereby He is able to subdue all things unto Himself" (Phil. 3:20-21). "For we that

are in this tabernacle do groan, being burdened: not for that we would be unclothed, but clothed upon, that mortality might be swallowed up of life" (2 Cor. 5:4).

It is expedient at this point to make specific reference to God's dealings with His chosen people, Israel. God initiated His particular relationship with Israel, first in the call of Abraham, where He declared that that people would be an everlasting nation and would possess an everlasting land (Gen. 12:1-3). In His dealings with King David, God enlarged the covenant with Israel to embrace an everlasting kingdom, with an everlasting throne and an everlasting King.

When their Messiah-King came to earth and identified Himself as such, He was rejected and crucified by the hierarchy of His own people, Israel. Their unbelief prevailed and their everlasting King returned to His Father in heaven. The fulfillment of His everlasting covenants with Israel were delayed but not abrogated.

At that time, God initiated His program with the Church. In the fulness of time (Eph. 1:10) His purposes with the Church will be completed, with the event described in the Scripture before us (1 Cor. 15:51-52). In theological terms, this event is spoken of as the Rapture. It will take place in the air (1 Thess. 4:13-18), where all the believers will meet the Lord and ascend with Him to heaven.

Following that, a short period of indescribable trouble and distress—sent by God in His wrath—will come upon those who remain on the earth. This is spoken of as "The Great Tribulation."

During that time of inexpressible suffering and death (Rev. chapters 6-18), God's earthly people will turn to the Lord and many will be saved. This is clearly foretold in Old Testament Scriptures like Jeremiah 31: 33-34. Zechariah wrote of that time: "And I [God] will pour out upon the house of David, and upon the inhabitants of Jerusalem, the spirit of grace and of supplica tions: and they [Israel] shall look upon Me whom they have pierced, and they shall mourn for Him, and shall be in bitterness for Him, as one that is in bitterness for his firstborn. In that day shall there be great mourning in Jerusalem . . ." (12:10-11).

In a recent issue of the *U. S. News and World Report,* Jefferey L. Sheller had a lengthy article on Eschatology. His polls show that sixty-one percent of Americans believe that Jesus Christ will return to the earth. Sixty percent believe that the Bible should be taken literally; forty-nine percent indicated that antichrist will come; forty-four percent believe that in the end times there will come the Battle of Armageddon; forty-four percent believe in the Rapture of the Church.

These are significant figures. In all this it is well always to keep in mind the words of our Lord who said, "But of that day and hour knoweth no man, no, not the angels of heaven, but My Father only" (Matt. 24:36). Christians do well to study the prophecies given in the Bible, but none should become prophets and try to set dates for these things to happen.

Many evangelicals believe that the Rapture (Christ's coming for the Church) is imminent and can occur on any day—morning, noon or night.

All these things will occur exactly according to *God's* timetable.

It is only fair to state that not all evangelical Christians believe precisely in this particular interpretation, and their views are regarded with respect.

"Put on incorruption... put on immortality"—This tells us that "corruption" and "mortality" will have been *put off* forever. "If immortality were not true," cried Tennyson in the hearing of James Knowles, "I'd sink my head tonight in a chloroformed handkerchief and have done with it all." But the word of Christ calms all fears and confirms all hopes: "If it were not so, I would have told you," our dear Lord declared (John 14:2).

"Death is swallowed up in victory"—The apostle refers to what is written in Isaiah 25:8. The swallowing up of "death" describes the complete removal of every trace of the physical effects that were brought about by Satan's power, by sin and by the curse. The word translated "victory," we are told, is one of the most beautiful terms in the Hebrew language. "It denotes the state of perfect inward rigour which excludes all possibility of outward decay, and hence: eternal duration" (F. Godet).

1 Corinthians 15:55-57

O death, where is thy sting?
O grave, where is thy victory?

The sting of death is sin;
and the strength of sin is the law.

But thanks be to God,
which giveth us the victory
through our Lord Jesus Christ.

"O death, where is thy sting . . .thy victory?"—An engaging shout of triumph over the ultimate enemy. This verse is an adaptation of Hosea 13:14, and the word rendered "grave" here is *Sheol* in Hosea. But *Sheol* ceased to exist for believers at the time of Christ's resurrection. Many translations have "death" in both parts of the verse, and, it would appear rightly so. It is death, not the grave, which gains victory over the bodily life. The grave is the depository of the body after death has gained the victory.

"The sting of death is sin"—It was on account of sin that death could strike man down fatally (Rom. 5:12). "The body is dead because of sin" (Rom. 8:10).

"The question of the corruptible one in the grave is: 'O grave, where is thy victory?' The question of the one living is: 'O death, where is thy sting?' " (Rev. Robert W. Teague).

"The strength of sin is the law"—What is it that gave sin this conquering power exercised by it? "The law" is the apostle Paul's answer. "Sin is not imputed where there is no law" (Rom. 5:13). Violation of God's law gives sin the "high-handed" character. The law makes sin an act worthy of capital punishment. "The throne of death thus rests on two bases: *sin*, which calls for condemnation, and *law*, which pronounces it" (F. Godet). "Blotting out the handwriting of ordinances that was against us, which was contrary to us, and took it out of the way, nailing it to His cross" (Col. 2:14).

Sin is vanquished and the law is disarmed in the substitutionary death and the resurrection of Christ.

"But thanks be to God, which giveth us the victory"— Sin brings curse and condemnation to us by the law. Since Christ's death has fulfilled the requirements of the law upon us (1 Pet. 2:24; 3:18), the power of sin is abolished and all the charges are dropped. The death of Christ in our stead has condemned sin and annulled the law, and His resurrection has swallowed up death.

We must, therefore, unceasingly give thanks to God for the Victor, our Lord and Savior, Jesus Christ.

The present tense of "giveth" signifies a constant, continuing process in which the believer gains the victory over sin in his daily life through the strength imparted by Christ.

> Ascend, beloved, to the feast;
> Make haste, thy day is come;
> Thrice blest are they the Lamb doth call
> To share the heavenly festival
> In the new Salem's palace-hall,
> Our everlasting home.
>
> —Horatius Bonar

* * *

In "For as in Adam all die . . ." the music changes suddenly from the A minor (sad) of the chorus to the D major of the accompanied recitative that follows "Behold, I show you a mystery." One can hear the mystery in the tones of the recitative.

"Behold, I show you a mystery . . ."—It seems that the music here is not fully up to Handel's standard. The trumpeter resonates in a complicated obligato[1] while the bass solo tells the story.

 "The trumpet shall sound"—Interestingly, the a cappella words on the previous recitative—the very last words—are "the last trump." In the bass aria, the first thing one hears is a trumpet solo. The trumpet is featured prominently throughout this piece.

"O death, where is thy sting?"—*Messiah's* only duet—an alto and tenor who render the Word of Scripture very effectively. The two voices combine to call out the glad questions. They set the stage for the joyful chorus that follows.

Biographers generally show little enthusiasm in this section of Scriptures, which afford such comfort for believers. What a blessed event when the redeemed will be transformed into the very likeness of the Redeemer.

"But thanks be unto God . . ."—Music of extraordinary intensity. Someone has called it, "glad, ascending victory chant."

---

[1] Obligato: an accompaniment that has its own character and importance.

Section 14

The Security
of the Redeemed

In the previous two sections the believers were positioned in heaven, rejoicing in all the glorious and eternal realities. All was so amazing, so wonderful, so utterly astounding, but can the believer really be *certain* of all this?

That is precisely the purpose of this section. The three Scriptures from Romans chapter eight concerning each and every believer are intended to bring full assurance, and cause every question and doubt to vanish.

Romans 8:31

What shall we then say to these things?
If God be for us,
who can be against us?

"What shall we then say to these things?"—"Things" refers not only to the immediate context but to all that the apostle had before presented as the basis of eternal salvation.

"If God be for us, who can be against us?"—The apostle

uses these questions "as pegs on which to hang this glorious paean of praise to God's sovereign grace." No doubt is implied by the question; it simply emphasizes a positive reality.

God is for us—believers—in foreknowledge, in foreordination, in calling, in justification and in glorification (Rom. 8:29-30). God is for us in all the immeasurable wealth of His redeeming power and His infinite grace. What else is there as specific proof that God is for us? It is stated in the next verse, He "spared not His Son, but delivered Him up for us all."

Since God is for us, then all our adversaries—though mighty and many—are of no account. Who can successfully oppose us? Who can hinder our salvation? Who can defeat the gracious purposes of God respecting us? God is our shield and defender. "The eternal God is thy refuge, and underneath are the everlasting arms" (Deut. 33:27). We need to lay hold of this truth so it becomes a conviction like that of Elisha: "Fear not, for they that be with us are more than they that be with them" (2 Kings 6:16).

We are not accustomed to absolute security in any area of life on the earth. In 1976, the U.S. airline industry had the safest year in its history. The 2,300 airliners flew 2.5 billion miles, carried 220 million passengers and only 45 people suffered death.

The passenger who shows his ticket to the smiling stewardess and buckles himself into his narrow seat has a 99.999 percent chance of arriving safely at his destination.

But every person who receives the blessed Lord Jesus as Savior has a 100 percent chance of arriving at his eternal destination. You cannot beat that. You cannot in any way undo what God has done when He redeemed you by His infinite grace because of His unfathomable love. "There is therefore now no condemnation to them who are in Christ Jesus" (Rom. 8:1).

Romans 8:33

Who shall lay any thing
to the charge of God's elect?
It is God that justifieth.

"Who shall lay any thing to the charge of God's elect?"—
Satan will try to do so, as he did with Job, but, as in the
case of Job, he will be vanquished in every charge that
he brings against any believer in Christ. Who can successfully bring a charge against God's chosen ones?
Who can turn God against them? The salvation of believers is not ascribed to anything—any good—in
themselves, but it is traced solely to the grace and
mercy of God, by whom "in love" they were chosen in
Christ before the foundation of the world (Eph. 1:4).

"What, though the accuser roar
of ills that I have done;
I know them well and thousands more;
Jehovah findeth none!"

"It is God that justifieth"—There is none that justifies
besides God. None can acquit a sinner from guilt and
pronounce him righteous, but God alone. "I, even I,
am He that blotteth out thy transgressions for Mine
own sake" (Isa. 43:25). Shall the God who justifies us,
condemn us? That is self-contradictory and utterly
impossible. If the highest court in the universe has no
charge to bring, then who can lay one against the believer in Christ? Since God justifies, He cannot
condemn.

The Bible says nothing of mere pardon. "There
can be no pardon except on the ground of satisfaction
of justice. It is by declaring a man just (that is, that justice in relation to Him is satisfied), that he is freed from
the penalty of the law, and restored to the favor of
God" (Charles Hodge).

"But we are bound to give thanks alway to God for you, brethren beloved of the Lord, because God hath from the beginning chosen you to salvation, through sanctification of the Spirit and belief of the truth; whereunto He called you by our Gospel to the obtaining of the glory of our Lord Jesus Christ" (2 Thess. 2: 13-14).

Both, God's decree of election and His pronouncement of justification, are irreversible!

"Our salvation is certain," said John Calvin, "because it is in the hand of God. Our faith is weak, and we are prone to waver: but God, who has taken us under His protection is sufficiently powerful to scatter with a breathe all the power of our adversaries. It is of great importance to turn our eyes to this."

Rest in the Lord, and give thanks for so great salvation!

Romans 8:34

Who is he that condemneth?
It is Christ that died, yea rather,
that is risen again,
who is even at the right hand of God
who also maketh intercession for us.

"Who is he that condemneth?"—Of course there is "the accuser of the brethren" (Satan) who is always ready to produce some damaging information. But God knows much more about His children because "He searcheth their hearts."

The answer is fourfold.

"It is Christ that died"—And He "died for our sins, according to the Scriptures" (1 Cor. 15:3). He died "the just for the unjust, that He might bring us to God" (1 Pet. 3:18). He paid sin's penalty in full. The account is settled. There is nothing now in the life of the believer worthy of condemnation. "There is therefore

now no condemnation to them who are in Christ
Jesus" (Rom. 8:1).

"Yea, rather, that is risen again"—The efficacy of His
substitutionary death resides in the reality of His resurrection. As the believer's sin was condemned in
Christ's death, so the believer's acquittal is pro-
nounced in Christ's resurrection.

Christ's resurrection is our certificate of justification (Rom. 4:25).

"Who is even at the right hand of God"—This is the
third ground of the believer's security. There can be
no condemnation because Christ has finished the
work of redemption and sits at God's right hand.

The Levitical priests never finished their work: it
was still imperfect and incomplete. In token of continued service, they *stood*, therefore, ministering daily.
But Christ, having offered one sacrifice for sins, by
which He hath perfected forever them that are sancti-
fied, sat down on the right hand of God (Heb. 10:12).

"Who also maketh intercession for us"—The protection afforded by our Lord's intercession saves every
believer to the uttermost. Calvin seeks to make clear:
"We must not think of Him as humbly supplicating
the Father on bended knee and with outstretched
hands." It must rather be understood as His claim that
the efficacy of His death is sufficient, and His intercession therefore is rather after the manner of His high
priestly prayer: "Father, I *will* that they also, whom
Thou hast given Me, be with Me where I am"
(Jn. 17:24).

We are unaccustomed in this life to have things
that last and endure. Thomas Edison (1847-1931)
invented the electric light bulb in 1879. Charles Kuralt
of the Columbia Broadcasting System tells a revealing
true story: In 1901, one of the newfangled gadgets was
hung and turned on in Livermore, California, Fire
Department. It's still there, and still on. The old bulb

has never been turned off in 71 years.

By today's standards it should have been replaced 852 times by now. The bulb, hand-blown, with a thick carbon filament, was made, it is said, by the Shelby Electric Company, which did not become one of the giants of the nation, for an obvious reason. The Shelby Company made light bulbs to last, and nobody ever re-ordered.

The bulb is accorded an awesome respect by Fire Captain Kirby Slate and his men.

God's redeeming work in the life of every believer is everlasting. The light of perfect salvation shines on and on and on—into endless eternity (Phil. 1:6).

The Lord is our advocate in glory, taking care of our need daily. It was in the light of this that Catherine Brettage, following a great conflict with Satan, said, "Reason not with me, I am but a weak woman; if thou hast anything to say, say it to Christ. He is my Advocate, my Strength, my Redeemer, and He will plead for me."

Praise God, "we have an advocate with the Father, Jesus Christ, the Righteous" (1 Jn. 2:1).

A preacher spoke with a lady who was troubled about her soul, "Well, how is it with you tonight; are you saved?" She said, "Oh, I don't know, Sir; I hope so." "Let me show you this verse," he said, " 'He that believeth on the Son hath everlasting life.' Do you believe on the Son?" "Oh, I do, Sir, I do believe on Him with all my heart." "Well, then, have you everlasting life?" "I hope so; I hope I have."

"Read the verse again," said the minister. She read, "He that believeth on the Son hath everlasting life." "Do you believe on the Son?" "I do." "Then, have you everlasting life?" "I certainly hope so. I do hope so."

"Well," he said, "I see what the trouble is." She said, "You do, what is the trouble?" "Why, when you were a girl they spelled very differently to what they did when I was a boy." "When you were a girl, h-a-t-h spelled *hope*; when I was a boy, h-a-t-h spelled *hath.*" She exclaimed, "Hath! 'He that believeth on the Son *hath* everlasting life.' Why, of course, I have it! Yes, I see it. I believe on the Son of God, and God says I *have* everlasting life." And so she entered into an "assurance forever."

* * *

 The last word of a mortal being in the oratorio has been spoken. The curtain separating time and eternity has fallen.

"If God be for us": One can hear a kind of intrigue in the strings following the question, "If God be for us?"

The assuring words in this section are rendered by a soprano solo in rhythmic relaxing style with the accompaniment of clear, melodic unison violins.

The encouraging words hold the attention of the believer here more than the music.

We are simply getting ready for the grand finale which will erupt in a moment.

Section 15

The New Song
of the Redeemed

The believers, having been assured of their security in Christ, are now seen in heaven again.

Background review: In Revelation, chapter 4, we read concerning the throne of grace in heaven where God and the Lamb are seated. The twenty-four elders —representing the vast body of believers—are seated on thrones round about the Throne of God. Each one wears a crown. In the midst and round about the throne are the four living creatures, "full of eyes." Each had six wings. Night and day, they are saying, "Holy, holy, holy, Lord God Almighty" (Rev. 4:1-8).

The twenty-four elders worship God and cast their crowns before the throne of God, saying, "Thou art worthy, O Lord, to receive glory and honor and power" (Rev. 4:10-11).

The nature of this scene leads us to believe that the body of Christ, the Church, had already been raptured to heaven.

The seven-sealed book that the apostle John saw *on* the hand of Him that sat on the throne contains all the details involved in securing the "redemption of the purchased possession," i.e., the bodies *and* souls of believers (Eph. 1:14).

An angel proclaimed loudly, "Who is worthy to open the book, and to loose the seals thereof?" (Rev. 5: 2). Who qualifies to take possession of the world and rule over it?

Adam, how about you? Wasn't the world given to you? Adam sorrowfully confesses, I forfeited my inheritance. I sinned it away.

John wept for there was no one qualified to open the book. Then one of the elders said, "Weep not; behold, the Lion of the tribe of Judah... hath prevailed to open the book, and to loose the seven seals" (Rev. 5: 5). John looked for the mighty lion, but he saw instead a "Lamb as it had been slain" (Rev. 5:6). The Lion of Judah's tribe is the Lamb of God. The Lion and the Lamb are one and the same. Had not Christ been the "Lamb," He could not now act as the "Lion." By His victory over death and all the strongholds of sin as the "Lamb," He acquired power which He can now exercise as the "Lion."

This picture of the Lord as a lion and yet also a lamb is surely one of the most paradoxical and wonderful in all of Scripture: powerful yet gentle, strong yet meek, fierce yet tender.

This is the One who shall execute the "judgments written" concerning the inhabitants of the earth, and forever vindicate God's ways. When Christ stood before Pilate, righteousness was on His side, but judgment was in the hands of a Roman governor. Now judgment is returned unto righteousness and the One who *is* righteous.

"And when He had taken the book, the living creatures and the four and twenty elders fell down before the Lamb, having every one of them harps and golden vials full of odors, which are the prayers of saints" (Rev. 5:8).

212

Revelation 5:9

And they sung a new song, saying,
Thou art worthy to take the book,
and to open the seals thereof:
for thou wast slain,
and hast redeemed us to God
by thy blood out of every kindred,
and tongue, and people and nation;

"And they sung a new song"—The song is new, not that Christ is new to them, but that the work of redemption is now being fully completed in every aspect and relationship. Christ is now assuming the character of a Lion on behalf of His earthly nation Israel and on behalf of all the redeemed.

"Thou art worthy to take the book and to open the seals" —In infinite love, He went to Golgotha and paid in full the great debt of sin. He redeemed the forfeited inheritance and set it free from Satan's dominion. Satan had been running things in this world to suit himself (2 Cor. 4:4), but his show is ended.

Thou art worthy, Oh Lord! Thou alone art worthy! Thou art infinitely worthy!

> " 'Worthy the Lamb that died,' they cry,
> 'To be exalted thus';
> 'Worthy the Lamb,' our lips reply,
> 'For He was slain for us.' "

"Out of every kindred, and tongue, and people and nation"—The Church is made up of people who are drawn to Christ from every tongue, from every nation in the whole world.

Meditate on these Scriptures, beloved, and with joy anticipate that great Day when we shall behold Him in all His glory and see how He "hast made us unto our God kings and priests: and we shall reign on the earth" (Rev. 5:10).

The wicked dead and all the unbelievers are not seen here. They will have their "day in court" at the White Throne Judgment, after the millennium, as recorded in Revelation 20:11-15.

Revelation 5:12

Saying with a loud voice,
Worthy is the Lamb that was slain to receive power,
and riches, and wisdom, and strength,
and honor, and glory, and blessing.

Notice the innumerable number of angels, the four living creatures and elders—numbering "ten thousand times ten thousand, and thousands of thousands" (Rev. 5:11).

And they are "saying with a loud voice: Worthy is the Lamb that was slain to receive:

"Power—Inherent omnipotent ability

"and riches—Undiminished, abounding wealth

"and wisdom—Unsearchable, unfathomable
knowledge

"and strength—Endowment of infinite resources

"and honor—Highest esteem; intrinsic excellence

"and glory—Absolute renown; unfolded fulness
of His deity

"and blessing"—Unending praise and adoration

Here is a sevenfold ascription of our Lord's absolute, incomparable perfection!

It is not that Christ lacked any of these things prior to this exaltation, but the accomplishment of redemption enables believers to perceive and value these infinite virtues in the Lord.

Angels in an outer circle join in "saying" this, but nowhere do we read of them singing except in Job 38, where they sang together when this world, in all its pristine excellence and beauty, sprang from the hand of God. That song was silenced by sin, and we never again read of angels singing. It is the redeemed that sing. As we have noted previously, the angels are not said to have *sung* at Christ's birth, as is popularly imagined.

Old John Bunyan says, "Oh this Lamb of God! He had a whole heaven to Himself, myriads of angels to do His pleasure, but this could not satisfy Him. He must have sinners to share it with Him."

Revelation 5:13

And every creature which is in heaven,
and on the earth, and under the earth,
and such as are in the sea,
and all that are in them, heard I saying,
Blessing and honor and glory and power,
be unto him that sitteth upon the throne,
and unto the Lamb for ever and ever.

"Every creature . . ."—Here is a scene that covers *all* creation. Every created being in heaven, on the earth, under the earth, in the sea—all of them. Included with men and angels is the lower creation—lions, giraffes, zebras, dogs, robins, whales, nightingales, butterflies, dolphins, eagles, buffaloes, porcupines and all the rest. This scene reveals the tremendous, indescribable event toward which the Father has been moving all the events in the history of creation—*the investiture of the Lord Jesus* with that inheritance of glory, honor, dominion and power—where "every knee should bow, of things in heaven, and things in earth, and things under the earth; and that every tongue should confess that Jesus Christ is Lord, to the glory of God

the Father" (Phil. 2:10-11). Let it be understood that here all will bow and acknowledge His place and majesty over all creation, though many will do so because they are commanded to do so and not because they love and adore Him. They do it because of coercion not devotion.

Here is what all of creation will declare on that day:

"Blessing,
and honor,
and glory,
and power,
be unto Him that sitteth upon the throne,
and unto the Lamb for ever and ever!" (Rev. 5:13)

Why are the bowls full of incense, which are the prayers of the saints (5:8), so closely connected with this occasion when the Lamb takes the book of the inheritance?

Is it possible that this great event was brought about through the prayers of saints, inspired of God, in accomplishing His great purpose of redemption? If so, then let us remember this as we pray. So often we think our prayers have little significance.

Let us conclude with the full-voiced expression of praise to God found in Psalm 98:1-4.

O sing unto the Lord a new song;
for He hath done marvellous things:
His right hand, and His holy arm,
hath gotten Him the victory.

The Lord hath made known His salvation:
His righteousness hath He openly showed
in the sight of the heathen.
He hath remembered His mercy and His truth
toward the house of Israel:
all the ends of the earth have seen

the salvation of our God.

Make a joyful noise unto the Lord,
all the earth:
make a loud noise, and rejoice, and sing praise.

* * *

 "Worthy is the Lamb . . ."—No chorus in the *Messiah* begins on a higher note. All four parts combine for this forceful entrance. "Blessing and honor" blend into the great "Amen."

The line is introduced by the sopranos, and soon thereafter the entire, energetic chorus takes it up in unrestrained praise and adoration of the Lamb of God that was slain.

This inspiring chorus, "Worthy is the Lamb," is probably second only to the Hallelujah Chorus in its effectiveness and popularity.

Gladness and joy pervade the chorus, "Worthy is the Lamb." It would seem necessary for the faces of the performers to have wide smiles! As with "For unto us a Son is born," the trumpets duplicate the melody pronouncement of the divine attributes—"Blessing and honor and glory and power be unto Him . . ." The choral pause after each title allows time for each ascription to sink in and to be appreciated.

Handel intended for this compound finale "to be the crowning achievement of the oratorio" (Lang). That it will forever remain the example and the envy of all choral composers, is the conviction of most Handel biographers and music critics.

The inspired words and the superior music together create an exalted, divinely charged atmosphere. Believers, engaged by thought and emotion, are deeply affected. They cannot help but ponder where they have come from and where they have arrived.

" 'Then I saw a Lamb, looking as if it had been slain.' A lamb! A helpless lamb, and a slaughtered one at that! Yet John in Revelation, and Handel in *Messiah,* sum up all history in this one mysterious image. The great God who became a baby, who became a lamb, who became a sacrifice—this God, who bore our stripes and died our death, this One alone is worthy. That is where Handel leaves us, with the chorus 'Worthy is the Lamb,' followed by an exultant Amen" (Philip D. Yancey, in *Christianity Today,* December 15, 1989).

John's closing thought in Revelation 22:20— "Even so, come Lord Jesus," should be ours as we joyfully anticipate our Lord's return.

"THE AMEN"

"And the four living creatures said, Amen"—(Rev. 5: 14). Dr. John F. Elliott, to whom a good measure of understanding of the holy Scriptures has been granted by the blessed Holy Spirit, made a careful study of the word "Amen," and here is his commentary:

"The ancient Hebrew word, 'Amen,' appears in the English translation of the Old Testament twenty-two times. In addition, the verb form of the word in Hebrew is used twenty-two times also, being translated 'believed.' In reverent and profane use, the word is in common parlance in the United States.

"For the New Covenant believer, the word comes to have sublime significance when we discover that our Lord Jesus reveals Himself as '. . . *The Amen*, the faithful and true witness, the beginning of the creation of God; . . .' (Revelation 3:14). On the basis of this unique revelation, the word comes to be very personal for the reverent Christian. With two exceptions in the four Gospels, the word 'Verily,' as used by our Lord would be properly translated 'Amen.' These instances should be regarded as the Messiah's signature. His signature appropriately appears at the end of each Gospel (Matthew, Mark, Luke and John). In John's Gospel Jesus is quoted as saying, 'Verily, Verily,' or 'Amen, Amen,' several times. However, in only one instance do His statements in John apply to the same truths to which He signs His Name in the other Gospels, Mark 9:12, and Luke 11:51.

"It ill behooves us to make use of His Names lightly, lest we blaspheme. This fact certainly applies to His
Name, 'Amen,' as well."

How well Handel understood the full meaning of
the word "Amen" is unknown, but he could not have
ended *Messiah* with any other word more suitable.
The oratorio closes with the "signature" of the Messiah
Himself —Amen.

* * *

The word "Amen" is sung in various
harmonies over forty times. The grand
finale is led off by the basses in a fugue
upon the Hebrew embracing term of devotion—AMEN.

Such a complete and beautiful review
of Messiah's glorious career ought not to
be over too suddenly.   Handel gives a
lengthy "Amen" in order to give the listeners time to
begin to assimilate the splendor of the Lord as revealed
in this musical presentation. Here again is the listeners' opportunity to claim the Messiah's work for themselves by adding their own hearty "Amen."

"In the monumental finale 'Amen Chorus,' notice
again the supreme skill with which Handel prepares
the first entry of the whole orchestra combining
trumpets and drums. Then the massive choral fugue...
All this is a fascinating combination of fugal grandeur
and structural surprise" (H. C. Robbins Landon).

In the course of the elaborate movement "the subject is divided, subdivided, inverted, enriched and
made subservient to many ingenious purposes of
harmony, melody and intonation with effects of which,
though all must be struck and delighted, yet those

only who are able to comprehend the whole merit of contexture [process of weaving parts into a whole] in this chorus, who have studied harmony or counterpoint are capable of judging of design, arrangements, contrivance and all the ingenious measures and perplexities of elaborate composition" (Charles Burney).

But whether or not the believer in the Redeemer understands all the brilliant contrivances of the composition, yet in his heart he will devotedly be participating in repeating   the Amen   and Amen and Amen!

Bibliography

As a rule, Handel biographers omit the name of the publisher, and we have followed their example. Feel free to call us if you desire name of publisher— 314/ 569-0244.

Alexander, Joseph Addison, *The Commentary on the Prophecies of Isaiah*, Grand Rapids, 1953.

Alford, Henry, *The Greek Testament*, Four Vols., Chicago, 1958.

Ammer, Christine, *The Harper-Collins Dictionary of Music*, New York, 1972.

Bairstow, Edward C., *Handel's Oratorio The Messiah*, London, 1928.

Bell, Arnold C., *Handel's Messiah*, London, 1923.

Bengel, Jn. Albert, *New Testament Word Studies*, Two Vols., Grand Rapids, 1971.

Benson, John A., *Handel's Messiah*, London, 1923.

Bindley, George, *The Larousse Encyclopedia of Music*, London, 1971.

Blom, Erich (ed.), *Grove's Dictionary of Music and Musicians*, Vols. 1, 3 & 5, New York, 1954.

Bloomfield, Arthur E., *All Things New*, Minneapolis, 1959.

Bonar, Horatius (ed.), *The Christian Treasury*, Edinburgh, 1862.

Bray, Anna Eliza, *Handel: His Life, Personal and Professional*, London. 1857.

Brown, Jn., *Exposition of the Epistle to the Hebrews*, Edinburgh, 1961.

Bullard, Roger A., *Messiah: The Gospel According to Handel's Oratorio*, Grand Rapids, 1993.

Bullinger, E. W., *The Companion Bible*, London, about 1900.

Burgh, Allatson, *Anecdotes of Music, Historical and Biographical*, London, 1814.

Burrows, Donald, *Handel: Messiah*, Cambridge, England, 1991.

_____, *Handel's Performance of Messiah*, Oxford, 1975.

Chalmers, Thomas, *Sermons and Discussions*, New York, 1881.

Chorley, Henry F., *The Messiah in Handel Studies*, London, 1859.

Chrysander, Friedrich, G. F. *Handel*, Leipzig, 1858.

Coxe, William H., *Anecdotes of G. F. Handel and John Christopher Smith*, London, 1799.

Crowest, Frederick J., *Handel and the English Music*, New York, 1909.

Cummings, William H., *Handel's Messiah*, 1903.

Dean, Winton, *Handel's Dramatic Oratorios*, London, 1959.

Deutsch, Otto, *Handel: A Documentary Biography*, New York, 1970.

Dwight, John S., *Handel and His Messiah* in *Dwight's Journal of Music*, London, 1853.

Epp, Theodore H., *Practical Studies in Revelation*, Lincoln, NE, 1969.

Ewen, David, *Twentieth Century Music*, Englewood Cliffs, NJ, 1959.

Exell, Joseph S. (ed.), *The Biblical Illustrator*, Grand Rapids, 1973.

Flower, Newman, *George Frideric Handel, His Personality and Times*, New York, 1923.

Gibbons, W. Francis, *The Unshakeable Kingdom*, London, 1949.

Godet, Frank, *Commentary on the Epistle to the Romans*, Grand Rapids, 1956.

_____, *Commentary on First Corinthians*, Grand Rapids, 1957.

_____, *Commentary on the Gospel of John*, Grand Rapids, 1886.

_____, *Commentary on the Gospel of Luke*, Grand Rapids, 1870.

Gore, Charles, *Epistle to the Romans*, London, 1900.

Gray, J. C. and G. M. Adams, *Gray and Adams Bible Commentary* Grand Rapids, date unknown.

Haldane, Robert, *Romans*, London, 1966.

Harrison, Norman B., *His Salvation*, Chicago, 1926.

Hastings, Rev. Edward (ed.), *The Speaker's Bible, Isaiah and Psalms*, Aberdeen, Scotland, 1935.

Hawkins, Sir John, *A General History of the Science and the Practice of Music*, Five Vols., London, 1776.

Herbage, Julian L., *Messiah*, New York, 1948.

Hodge, Charles A., *A Commentary on the Epistle to the Romans*, Philadelphia, 1836.

Hogwood, Christopher, *Handel*, New York 1988.

Hoste, W. *Studies in Bible Doctrine*, London, 1948.

Hurdis, James, *The Village Curate*, London, 1788.

Ironside, Harry A., *Expository Notes on the Prophet Isaiah*, Neptune, NJ, 1952.

_____, *Lectures on the Revelation*, New York, 1930.

Jacobi, Peter, *The Messiah Book*, New York, 1982.

Jennings, F. C., *Studies in Isaiah*, Neptune, NJ, 1935.

Keates, Jonathan, *Handel: The Man and His Music*, New York, 1985.

Keil, C. F. and F. Delitzsch, *Commentary on the Old Testament*, Ten Vols., Grand Rapids, 1975.

Kelly, William, *An Exposition of Isaiah*, Oak Park, IL, 1975.

Kennedy, Michael, *The Concise Oxford Dictionary of Music*, New York, 1985.

Landon, H. C. Robbins, *Handel and His World*, Boston.

Lang, Paul Henry, *George Frederic Handel*, New York, 1966.

Lange, John Peter (ed.), *Lange Commentary on the Holy Scripturess.* Vols. on *Psalms* and *Revelation*, Grand Rapids.

Langhorne, John, *The Tears of Music: A Poem to the Memory of Mr. Handel*, London, 1760.

Larsen, Jens Peter, *Handel's Messiah*, London, 1957.

_____, *Handel's Messiah*, New York, 1972.

Lenski, R. C. H., *Interpretation of Romans and Revelation*, Columbus, OH, 1943.

Luckett, Richard, *Handel's Messiah*, New York, 1992.

MacFarren, George A., *Messiah: An Analysis of the Oratorio*, London 1857.

Mainwaring, John, *Memoirs of the Life of the Late George Frideric Handel*, Published anonymously, London, 1760.

Maxwell, J. Brian, *Handel's Messiah: Dispelling the Sacred Illusion.* An unpublished thesis, Dallas, TX 1980.

Monser, Harold E. (ed.), *The Cross Reference Bible*, Grand Rapids, 1959.

Morgan, G. Campbell, *Studies in the Four Gospels*, Old Tappan, NJ, 1927.

Morison, James, *A Practical Commentary on the Gospel According to St. Matthew*, Boston, 1884.

Motyer, J. Alec, *The Prophecy of Isaiah*, Downer's Grove, IL. 1993.

Moule, H. C. G., *Studies in Romans*, Grand Rapids, 1977.

Myers, Robert Manson, *Handel's Messiah*, New York, 1948.

Newell, William R., *The Book of Revelation*, Chicago, 1941.

The New Encyclopedia Britannica. Vol. 8 and Vol. 14, Chicago, 1973.

The New Lexicon Webster's Dictionary, New York, 1987.

Newton, John, *The Works of the Reverend John Newton*, two vols., Philadelphia, 1831.

Olsen, Erling C., *Meditation in the Psalms*, New York, 1939.

Ottman, Ford C., *The Unfolding of the Ages*, Grand Rapids, 1967.

Parker, Joseph, *The People's Bible*. Vols. on *Psalms, Job* and *Matthew*, London, 1850.

Perowne, J. J. Steward, *The Book of Psalms*, two vols., Grand Rapids, 1966.

Pink, Arthur W., *Exposition of the Gospel of John*, Grand Rapids, 1945.

Plumer, William S., *Commentary on Romans*, Grand Rapids, 1971.

_____, *Psalms*, Edinburgh, 1867.

Price, Walter K., *Revival in Romans*, Grand Rapids, 1962.

Ramsay, Dean Edward B., *Two Lectures on the Genius of Handel and the Distinctive Character of His Sacred Compositions*, Edinburgh, 1862.

Randel, Don Michael, *The New Harvard Dictionary of Music*, Cambridge, MA, 1986.

Rockstro, William S., *The Life of George Frideric Handel*, London, 1883.

Sadie, Stanley, *Handel*, London, 1968.

Schaeffer, Francis A., *How Shall We Then Live?*, Westchester, IL, 1976.

Scholes, Percy A., *The Puritans and Music*, London, 1934.

Scroggie, W. Graham, *The Psalms*, Westwood, NJ, 1948.

Seiss, J. A., *The Apocalypse*, Grand Rapids, 1966.

_____, *Lectures on Hebrews*, Grand Rapids, 1954.

Sheppard, Gerald T. (ed.), *The Geneva Bible*, original in 1602, New York, 1989.

Spence, H. D. M. (ed.), *The Pulpit Commentary*
on *Isaiah* and *Psalms*, Chicago.

Spurgeon, Charles H., *Sermons on the Book of Revelation*,
Grand Rapids, 1962.

_____, *The Treasury of David*, London, 1904.

Streatfeild, Richard A., *Handel*, London, 1909.

Thompson, Oscar, *The International Encyclopedia of Music
and Musicians*, New York, 1975.

Vine., W. E., *Epistle to the Romans*, Grand Rapids, 1965.

Weinstock, Herbert, *Handel*, 1946.

Wheeler, Opal, *Handel at the Court of Kings*, New York 1943.

Wuest, Kenneth S., *Wuest's Word Studies - Hebrews*,
Grand Rapids, 1956.

Young, Percy, *Handel*, New York, 1963.

Biography Index

228

230

Commentary and Music Index

Scripture Index